# eBay

# The 3rd 100 Best
## Things I've Sold on

# eBay

## My Story Continues
### by The Queen of Auctions
# Lynn A. Dralle

## "The Cash Registers
## are Still Ringing"

# All Aboard, Inc.

# Preface

I get emails every day thanking me for writing these *100 Best* books. I have to say that they are truly a labor of love. As I start my journey writing the third book in the series, I realize that my life has changed quite a bit since I started writing the first book back in 2003.

For one thing, it has become much easier to write. I guess publishing those free ezines (www.queensbonus.com) every week has helped to hone my writing skills. As most of you know, I never planned on being a writer. It is funny where life takes you, if you just give it a chance.

Another change is that I really have my Dralle listing method polished and it works for me and thousands of others. I can find and list 100 unique items each and every week in about fifteen hours. Being so dialed in gives me the time I need to write and do other things I enjoy, like travel.

I am sitting on a balcony in the West Caymans composing this preface. My life has always been good, but now it is incredibly great. eBay has given me the opportunity to live life the way I want to. It truly is a way for anyone to have the American Dream of business ownership.

I started writing these *100 Best* books to honor my grandmother. That has not changed and I try to infuse as much of her spirit into these pages as I can. She has been gone seven years now and it is not as difficult as it was when I wrote the first one in 2003. I don't cry every day now when I think about her, only sometimes. What I have learned is that time does heal your heart

I hope you have as much fun reading these new 100 stories as I had writing them. I wish great success to you in your eBay business and more importantly, happiness in your life.

eBay with
♡ Heart
Lynn

First Edition 2007

ISBN-10: 0-9768393-1-8
ISBN-13: 978-0-9768393-1-6

For more information write:

All Aboard, Inc.
P.O. Box 14103
Palm Desert, CA 92255

Lynn@TheQueenofAuctions.com
www.TheQueenofAuctions.com

Designed by: Lee Dralle (LDralle.com), Becky Raney
and Lynn A. Dralle
Edited by: Susan Thornberg

Printed in the United States of America
Print & Copy Factory
4055 Irongate Road
Bellingham, WA 98226
www.printcopyfactory.com

This book is dedicated to
Lee Dralle

The best graphic artist, photographer, uncle, and brother ever!
Thank you for helping to make my business the success that it has
become and for not rolling your eyes too many times—especially
when things have to be finished right now—like this book!

# Acknowledgments

My greatest thanks to:
Cheryl Leaf
Lee Dralle
Susan Thornberg
Becky and Larry Raney
Houston and Indiana
Sharon Chase
Wayne and Sue Dralle
Kristin Dralle
Melanie Souve
Peter Gineris
Maureen Arcand
Krystal Garcia
eBay
My book and ezine readers
My eBay students
AND all our great eBay customers!

# Contents

## Introduction

## The 3rd 100 Best...eBay Ka-Ching!

## Afterword

# Introduction

## Grandma

It was in November of 1950 in Bellingham, Washington, that my grandmother opened her antiques and gift store on the corner of Northwest and Illinois. It was originally painted pink with turquoise trim. How 1950s Eames era! It would remain open for 52 years.

"Cheryl Leaf Antiques, Gifts & Coins" was the name of her original 200-square-foot shop, and over the years, the building (which also housed her living quarters) would eventually grow to 8,000 square feet. It was filled from floor to rafters with treasures she had acquired abroad, through "wanted" ads, from walk-in customers, from other dealers, and from buying entire estates. My grandmother never went to garage sales. Fast forward to today, where I make my living going to garage sales and selling what I find on eBay.

But back to Cheryl Leaf, my mentor, grandmother and best friend. She was one of the smartest business people I have ever met and I learned so much from her. She worked extremely hard in her business. It was her passion. She would get up at 5:00 a.m. every morning and often work until midnight or one a.m. She also exhibited at between twelve and eighteen antiques shows a year, and spent a lot of time on the road.

I grew up working for my grandmother. She would take me to antiques shows when I was a little girl, and I worked for her most days after school and on weekends. My grandmother was one of those people who always had a twinkle in her eye and loved life. Every day was an adventure to her. I left Bellingham to live in Los Angeles in 1981. I think that was very hard on her.

In January of 1993, she fell and broke her hip. I flew up from Los Angeles to visit her in the hospital. We celebrated her 81st birthday in the old St. Luke's Hospital with a cardboard cake covered with tin foil and 81 candles. We almost burned down the place. I can still see the shocked and scared look on her face when the doctor told her she would have to go to a nursing home to recover. My grandmother never wanted to end up in a nursing home. It was her worst fear.

I flew back home to Los Angeles with a lot on my mind. After some serious soul searching I called my grandmother and asked her if she would give me a job running the store. Of course! She was overjoyed. She could only pay me $10 an hour and I was making about $27 an hour in LA. I decided it was time to sell my townhouse and move back to Bellingham. Those last few years that I would get to spend with her were priceless, and worth a lot more than the $17 an hour difference. We all knew that getting her healed and out of the nursing home and back to her business was very important in keeping her alive. I ran the store from April 1993 (when we brought her back home to live) until it closed in August of 2002.

Running the store with my grandmother was not work—it was play. She always believed in me and told me that I could do and be anything I dreamed of being. I miss those days, and I miss my grandmother.

## eBay

I started buying on eBay for the shop in 1998 after we lost our franchise with Ty (the maker of Beanie Babies) and I needed stock to replace those sales. I was intimidated by the thought of selling on eBay and stayed away as long as possible, but my grandmother got sick in 1999 and we had to raise a lot of money quickly for her nursing care expenses.

We jumped in, and with all of my grandmother's inventory, we were selling $20,000 a month before we knew it. Once I got started selling, I couldn't stop. I was hooked. I don't think I have taken more than four weeks off from selling on eBay since 1999. I still put 100 new items on each week.

When my grandmother passed away in 2000, It took another two years to liquidate the store. There was just so much stuff. At the end, we divided up the eBay-worthy items that remained into four portions for the inheritors: me, my brother Lee, my sister Kristin (Kiki), and my mom Sharon. Each inheritor would be responsible for disposing of his or her own items.

I was in the shop one day and a customer asked me, "When are you going to end this painful liquidation process?" I said, "I don't know, but my grandmother always told me it would take two years." I had my answer. We closed the doors to my grandmother's brick-and-mortar store on August 2, 2002—exactly two years from the day she died. It was a sad day.

The beauty of eBay is that it allows me to live anywhere. I had been back in Bellingham almost ten years at that point, and I was missing southern California. I realized that I didn't have to stay in the Pacific Northwest, and in October of 2002, my kids and I moved to Palm Desert.

## The 100 Best Things I've Sold on eBay

About six months after arriving in California, I decided I wanted to write a book honoring my grandmother. I had started writing it focusing on the hundred most important things I had learned from her, but it was slow going. In September of 2003, I was teaching a class about eBay for The Learning Annex in Los Angeles. I told a story about an Edwardian mourning case (see #74 in *The 100 Best Things I've Sold on eBay*) that I'd sold earlier in the year. One of the women in the class yelled out, "That story gave me goosebumps!" My stories were her favorite part of the entire three-hour class. Wow! I knew that I had *lots* of stories to tell about my eBay successes (and failures).

After hearing my student's "goose-bumps" comment, I realized that I could combine my eBay stories and my grandmother's lessons into a single book. I could use my eBay experiences as a framework for my grandmother's story—the lessons she taught me, the stories she told, the life she lived. I was excited! When I started writing that book, I couldn't stop! That book is *The 100 Best Things I've Sold on eBay,* and it is the first in this series. Every day I get an email from someone that has read *The 100 Best,* and they tell me what an inspiration it has been to them. That warms my heart.

## More 100 Best Things I've Sold on eBay— Money Making Madness

By 2006 I had acquired another 100 great items for a book, and I started writing *Money Making Madness*. Those two years in between books were quite a learning experience! When I first started, eBay wasn't as user-friendly as it is now. I also found that I had to re-learn everything that I had been taught in the antiques store. Things that would sell in our shop in Bellingham, WA, didn't always bring much on eBay, if they sold at all. On the flip side, things that I wouldn't ever consider stocking in our store sold for big bucks on eBay—things like empty vintage cereal boxes, skateboards and insulators. The *100 Best* books give me the opportunity to share many of the lessons I've learned with readers in a fun and entertaining format.

*Money Making Madness,* the second book in the series, contains stories about more items that I actually had to go out and buy than the first *100 Best* book does. The items described in *Money Making Madness* weren't just handed to me by my grandmother. That is one reason the second book is so fun. I was scared at first to leave the shop and see if I really could make a living by going to garage sales—which is the complete opposite of how my grandmother got her stock. I am happy to report that it is working out incredibly well for me. In fact, the items that I have sold on eBay for the most money are not things I inherited, but things I bought at garage and estate sales for $2 to $20.

## The 3rd 100 Best Things I've Sold on eBay—Ka-Ching

*Money Making Madness* ended with a toaster that I sold on May 8, 2005. So, in early 2007 I realized that I had another two years' worth of sales to start sifting through for my third *100 Best* book.

I didn't actually start writing this one until late February, and I really put the pressure on myself, my brother Lee, my printer Becky, and my editor Susan. We had a target publishing date of July 7, 2007. 777. I thought that would be really cool! We will make it, but just by the skin of our teeth. Lee, Becky and Susan are awesome to work with and I want to say a big thank you to them!!!

This book contains stories about a lot of kooky things that you may overlook at garage and estate sales. It also doesn't have the huge dollar sales that *Money Making Madness* did (three items in that book sold for over $2,000). My most expensive sale of a single item in this book is $1,125. The big hits are becoming fewer and farther apart. But that is consistent with what I have always taught: you make your money selling $18 items (that is my average sales price) day in and day out. If you sit around and wait for the home runs instead of taking the base hits, you won't be able to pay your bills.

There are a lot of fun stories in this book and I had a blast writing it. It ends with a horse saddle that I sold on July 9, 2006, so you may just see another one of these books next year. I don't know, call me crazy, but I really enjoy writing them. I especially love Diane's quote on the back of the book: "HURRY HURRY." When she heard I was almost finished with book number three, she emailed me to beg for number four. We will see how it goes. Yikes!

The title of this book comes from a contest offered to the 10,000 readers of my ezine. Thank you, Stephanie O'Leary! *Ka-Ching* was perfect. Even though we don't use real cash registers anymore and don't get to hear that wonderful sound, I still remember it from the shop. It was one of my grandmother's favorite sounds also! Of course! So, welcome to *Ka-Ching!*

# #1  Cugat Make Love Not War

**Make Love Not War Oil Painting Signed Xavier Cugat 1960**

**Description:**
Make Love Not War Painting is signed Xavier Cugat 1960. A humorous and famous painting by Xavier Cugat measures 10" by 8" and with the frame measures 14¼" by 12¼". Tag on the back says "No. 21856 Bin 5027." In great condition with a tiny chip on the frame. Cugat was a famous Spanish bandleader who also painted.

**Winning Bid:**

**$89.00**

**Ended:** 5/28/05
**History:** 16 bids
**Starting Bid:** $9.99
**Winner:** Atlanta, GA

**Viewed**
000125 X

# Cugat Make Love Not War  #1

## The Story

You would think that I would have learned by now. But no. There I was at an estate sale in Palm Desert in the garage looking at a HUGE oil painting with a sign on it that said "RARE PAINTING $50." I am a sucker for the word RARE and I still dream of hitting the jackpot with an oil painting. You know the ones you have heard about that sell for millions. I asked the family having the sale to tell me the back story.

"Well, this was purchased many years ago from a very famous store. It was very expensive when it was new. If you buy it, you can call us on Monday after we find out the name of the store from our aunt." It was all sounding wonderfully perfect. I could just picture my bank account full of money and my imminent retirement. "I'll take it."

As I was leaving, I noticed a small oil painting of a naked cartoon couple. It looked intriguing. It was only five dollars. And it was tiny. Maureen (my assistant) would hate me for the large painting, so I knew that I had better buy something small to balance it out. "I'll take that, too."

Well, Monday rolled around and with anticipation I dialed the number on the business card they had given me. The gentleman told me with pride in his voice that the painting had been purchased at Pier One.

My boat had sailed, the millions were gone, and I wasn't going to be retiring any time soon. I didn't even bother to put that painting on eBay. It sat in my entryway (the one my mother now calls "the lobby" since my eBay business has taken over my house) for the last year. I finally moved it out to the garage about two weeks ago.

The silver lining in all of this is that the small cartoon painting turned out to be an original oil painted by Xavier Cugat in 1960. My research told me that it was worth $100, so I decided to donate 10% of the sale price to my favorite charity—Toys for Tots. I try to do this whenever I get a $100 item. Always give back when you can, and eBay makes it soooo easy.

Cugat was a famous Spanish bandleader known as "Cugy." He was born in Spain and was taken to Cuba by his parents at the age of four. He was a child prodigy and violin virtuoso. His music career brought him international fame. He always had a pad and pencil, however, that he carried along with his violin. He was a true artist and was even a cartoonist for the LA Times. The painting that I had was a great example of his work.

The Cugat ended up selling for $89, Toys for Tots got a donation, and I still own the huge RARE painting. Oh, well. Maybe someday it will get put on eBay. I just can't bear the thought of shipping it.

# #2  Face Vase Decanter

$1.00 Paid
From: Garage sale

**Face Vase Decanter Eames Era Hoglund Kosta Boda? Blenko**

**Description:**
There are no maker's marks on this neat decanter. I believe it to be Eames era circa 1950s to 1970s. It is olive green and 9¾" tall. I would love to know who the maker is—we have guessed at a few (Hoglund, Kosta Boda, Blenko) but would definitely say Scandinavian. The stopper plastic is breaking. No chips no cracks. In great shape.

**Winning Bid:** **$33.00**

Ended: 5/29/05
History: 10 bids
Starting Bid: $9.99
Winner: Dubuque, IA

Viewed
000189 X

# Face Vase Decanter  #2

## The Story

I love buying $1 items. There is no risk (unlike $50 RARE paintings). Whenever I look at an item and am considering its purchase, I always ask myself this question: "Is it worth $10?" If so, I snap it up.

I had seen decanters like this one in my house when I was growing up. My mom loved (and still does love) all that mid-century Scandinavian glass. This one was olive green, a color that is usually associated with the 1970s. The problem and the challenge with glassware from this era is that most of it wasn't marked. If it did leave the factory with a mark, it was usually a sticker that would eventually be taken off.

That is why I put three different makers' names in the title. The two Scandinavian ones are Hoglund and Kosta Boda. The American one is Blenko. I thought the vase had the highest probability of being Hoglund.

It was right around this time in my life when I got the contract to write *The Unofficial Guide to Making Money on eBay* for John Wiley. Wiley is a huge publishing house and it was a great opportunity to write a basic "how to." They wanted the book to be completed by August for a December 2005 release. That was going to be a heck of a lot of writing in a very short four-month period. Why not? I like a challenge.

My mother is always telling me that if I don't have a huge project going on—a house remodel, a new book, or a new product launch—it will just be a matter of minutes (or seconds) until I overcommit myself again! It does make life interesting in my house.

This is a lesson that I definitely learned from Cheryl Leaf (my grandmother). Her house and the attached antique store were always a whirlwind of activity. Everyone congregated in the shop to hang out and help with the business. There was always some type of project being worked on—whether it was pricing a huge new shipment of gift items, sorting through an entire estate, or making jewelry. As she always used to say, "Never a dull moment."

I don't think that you can write about how to make a living selling on eBay unless (of course) you are still doing it. That is why I still put 100 new items each week on eBay and average about $10,000 a month in sales. My average sticker price is about $18, so I am always looking for these $1 items that will turn into at least $10. You make a consistent living selling $18 items, not $1,000 items. Those are few and far between.

This decanter ended up selling for about double my average ticket price—$33—so I was very happy.

**Never a Dull Moment!**

# #3  Clown Purse

**$10.00**
Paid
From: Garage sale

**RARE Vintage Clown Purse Needlepoint Eames Circus SUPER**

**Description:**
This is an awesome purse. Great for a clown collector to use or display. It is in such great condition. The needlepoint is in amazing shape. The leather portion is worn. The inside of the purse is also in great condition. 10½" by 17" (to the handle) by 3". Such a neat rare piece. I would guess 1940s to 1950s Eames era retro.

**Winning Bid:** **$102.50**

Ended: 5/29/05
History: 9 bids
Starting Bid: $9.99
Winner: Chicago, IL

**Viewed**
000162 X

# Clown Purse #3

## The Story

For some reason I am drawn to clown items. I think there is a huge population of clown collectors and that eBay is where they go to get their fixes. Phyllis Diller has a quote about clowns that really got me thinking: "You've got to realize that when all goes well, and everything is beautiful, you have no comedy. It's when somebody steps on the bride's train, or belches during the ceremony, that you've got comedy!"

It is so true. Clowns make comedy out of tragedy, and if life were perfect, we wouldn't ever see humor. Humor has its roots in our mistakes.

I saw this purse at a garage sale and couldn't believe that the lady holding the sale wanted $10 for it. $10 is a lot of money for a garage sale item. Still, there was just something about it that sucked me in. I hemmed and hawed over it for quite some time. I finally reasoned to myself that the worst thing that could happen would be that it would just sell for my $9.99 starting bid. No harm, no foul. And it might make a good story someday!

The week I listed the clown purse was a very exciting time in my life. I had just been in LA filming an episode for "Inside Edition" with Deborah Norville. The segment was "Things you should never buy used," and the camera crew had followed me around to Santa Monica thrift stores to film me buying used shoes, worn-out mattresses, recalled car seats, and unsafe baby cribs.

A purse is a fine thing to buy used—another reason I sprang for the clown bag. Some of the stuff that I found in the thrift stores, however, was disgusting. We even found a used jock strap, but "Inside Edition" didn't air the footage on that item. Too bad—it would have made a humorous piece! But "Inside Edition" wants to be considered a hard-hitting news show, and jock strap exposés apparently don't fit that profile.

I do have a photo of the jock strap on the table of items that we hauled back to the production offices. Disgusting! It was a fun day of filming and the episode aired on May 28th. It was a blast to watch it with my family, and my kids got a kick out of seeing their "mommy" on TV.

So while this was all going on, 162 people viewed that clown purse and it sold for over $100. My purchase had not turned into a tragedy!

# #4  IBM Charting Templates

**$0.⁴⁰ Paid**

**From:** Church rummage sale

**4 Early IBM Charting Templates Form X24 884 6 Unusual**

**Description:**
4 Early IBM charting templates Form X24 884 6 Unusual.

**Winning Bid:** **$12.⁵⁰**

**Viewed**
000041 X

**Ended:** 5/31/05
**History:** 2 bids
**Starting Bid:** $6.99
**Winner:** Apple Valley, CA

# IBM Charting Templates #4

## The Story

You may have noticed that over the years my auction descriptions have gotten shorter and shorter. Sometimes all I do is just copy the auction title and paste it into the description box. On this auction, I forgot to even list the dimensions or condition. Occasionally I do that when I am in a hurry, and amazingly this item sold even without that information.

I had picked these up at a garage sale for ten cents each. I bought them because they reminded me of the type of things that my grandfather (Elmer Leaf) kept around his office. My grandfather was an architect and he also taught school—aeronautics. His office in the back of my grandmother's antique store would eventually become my office when I moved home to run the shop.

The office was the neatest room, right off of the old kitchen. It had shelves galore and a nice window that looked out onto a big tree. We had played house under that tree when we were growing up, using old tin dishes and making mud pies. I have such good memories of that place, and the office felt like home.

Another reason I liked to sneak into my grandfather's office was because he always had bags of candy hidden up high in those shelves. He was the nicest and gentlest man you can imagine. He used to walk with my brother and I up to Yeager's (a local store) and give us each a dollar to spend on sticker books. Those were the days, and my memories of that period will last a lifetime.

My grandfather became ill with Alzheimer's at a fairly young age. I remember not really understanding what was going on; I was only twelve when he died. During his illness I used to pile all his hats on his head (eight of them), and even though he didn't have all his wits about him, he still played along with the joke. He was such a good sport and loved my brother, sister, and I a lot. I know that he would have loved his great-grandkids. Unfortunately, they came along more than twenty years after his death.

My grandmother was only 64 when he died and she lived another 24 years without him. She missed my grandfather a lot. I can't imagine being alone for 24 years, but she said that no one could ever replace him. They had gotten married when she was twenty and he was 27. Unfortunately, you just don't find many marriages that last a lifetime like that anymore.

But back to those templates. They were made by IBM, and I don't know what they were used for. However, being vintage and I guess in some type of demand, they ended up selling for $12.50. A great return on a 40-cent investment, thanks to the memories of my grandfather and our shared office.

# #5 LucasArts Sam & Max

$1.00 Paid

From: Garage sale

**Sam Max Hit the Road PC CD IBM Lucas Arts Vintage MI**

## Description:

*Sam and Max* is mint in box or mint in package. This is still in the original plastic. Amazing and hard to find in this condition. ISBN 2327210618. *Sam and Max Hit the Road,* the classic-est *Sam and Max* game of them all. You play Sam (a canine shamus) and Max (a hyperkinetic rabbity thing), the freelance police. Travel all over the US on the trail of a sasquatch named Bruno kidnapped from his place at the Hall of Oddities, and on the way visit locations like the World's Largest Ball of Twine, The World of Fish, and the Mount Rushmore Dinosaur Tarpit. The game involves some of the most twisted humor in a Lucasarts adventure game, and the dialogue including a non-sequitur option goes way over the top. *Sam & Max* is not entirely an adventure game—every once in a while there'll be an action sequence like Wak-A-Rat. They encounter strange locations, entirely unhelpful clues, a cast of suspicious (or possibly just dim) characters, and a number of plot twists that complicate their mission. *Sam and Max Hit the Road* still remains a favorite of gamers today.

**Winning Bid:**

# $46.66

**Ended:** 6/03/05
**History:** 10 bids
**Starting Bid:** $9.99
**Winner:** Sandy, UT

**Viewed**

000110 X

# LucasArts Sam & Max  #5

## The Story

So just when I comment on not writing a lot in my auction descriptions, I go ahead and write a novel. Well, it was important information. I had always heard about vintage software and video games selling for a lot, so I had been wanting to try it.

I found this computer game at a garage sale still in the original plastic. Original plastic is always a great idea—especially for books, records and video games. I don't think it is such a great idea for couches—especially if you are using them in your home. If this is you, please, please take the plastic off!

What is really cool is that some of the new video game platforms, like the Wii that my kids got from Santa, actually encourage them to get up off one of my eight couches! (I collect couches—none of them with plastic covers!)

However, with a mint in box (MIB) or mint in plastic (MIP) item that you are going to sell on eBay, never remove the plastic. You can quote me on that and take that tip to the bank.

What really intrigued me about the description of the game (lifted from the back side) was the word "non-sequitur." Even though I am now an author (and have written eight or nine books) I still don't know the meanings of some words. I had an idea about this one, but thought I had better do some research.

A non-sequitur is "a humorously absurd comment which has no relation to the comment it follows; a statement so foolish or illogical that it can not be responded to." OK, that makes sense for a high-brow type of video game.

And that was just one of the reasons that there was a huge following for the original *Sam and Max* game. It was originally released back in 1993 by Lucasarts. I found out that it enjoys legendary status in the hallowed halls of PC gaming. Who knew? But great news for me.

The founder of Lucasarts, it turns out, is none other than George Lucas. George is a fellow USC alumni and an amazing filmmaker. I am sure that you have heard of him and maybe one of his films, "American Graffiti," "Star Wars," or "Raiders of the Lost Ark"?

With the money from American Graffiti and Star Wars, Lucas was able to open Lucasfilm Games in Marin County in May of 1982. The name was later changed to Lucasarts. *Sam and Max Hit the Road* was based on a pair of comic book characters originally created by Steve Purcell, and it quickly became a best seller.

It became a best seller for me on eBay and I still look for any mint-in-plastic gaming items when out and about. But I wouldn't touch a mint-in-plastic couch with a ten foot pole (one of my grandmother's favorite sayings, and possibly a non-sequitur!) Or am I way off base?

# #6 Hawaiian Mask

**$3.00** Paid
**From:** Thrift store

## Hawaii Hawaiian Tiki Wall Mask Bamboo WEIRD

**Description:**
This is a very strange and unique piece. It is some type of wall mask and it is very, very heavy. The curly hair and beard are a natural part of the wood. I would guess 1960s or so. Eames era. 17" by 7½". If anyone knows anything about it we would appreciate knowing! Thanks. In pretty good to very good condition.

**Winning Bid:**

# $46.51

**Ended:** 6/07/05
**History:** 23 bids
**Starting Bid:** $9.99
**Winner:** Midland, OR

**Viewed**
000211 X

# Hawaiian Mask #6

## The Story

I have always been drawn to masks, and it is probably because my grandmother collected them. Of course—it all goes back to Cheryl Leaf. On the wall outside of her tiny kitchen was where her mask collection lived.

For many cultures, the power of the mask lies in its origin as a living thing. Masks are created for specific reasons, such as to ensure a good crop or to increase fertility. Many masks (and the ones that I collect) are carved from wood. The carver believes that because the tree was once alive, its spirit will carry on into the mask. Wow!

My grandmother's mask collection was very cool; I grew up wondering where the masks came from and what they were used for. Some of them were really scary, like the dark Swedish one that had been blackened over a fire, and the really big African ones that were long and pointy. Over the years, I was given many of her masks as Christmas and birthday presents.

Fast forward to two years ago. I owned my grandma's entire mask collection, and it was proudly displayed over the fireplace in my rec room (also known as "the eBay room"). When we moved my shipping department into the eBay room from the garage, the mask collection had to go to make way for the bubble wrap and packing peanut dispensers.

I plan to hang them in my new office, but I just haven't found the time to do it yet. For now, they sit, patiently waiting for me to get my act together. But don't fear, the spirits of my masks are safe. And luckily, I have a photo of them before they were taken down to share with you.

I found the mask sold in this auction in my favorite thrift store for $3. I won't pass up a good mask any time it is under $10. I thought that it looked to be Hawaiian, and artifacts from Hawaii are always collectible. The woman who bought the mask emailed me the greatest story.

> When I was small (I am 51 now), my older brother carved a tiki mask out of palm wood, and it hung in our home forever. When I opened my karate school in 2002, my father let me have that mask to put up on the wall for decoration. Over the years, I have added similar masks to the wall and I get a lot of compliments. I am Filipino with Hawaiian heritage, so my home and karate school reflect that. Mahalo, Robyn.

How cool is that? The masks that Robyn have not only embrace her heritage, but the spirit of each mask guards her home and business—just as my grandmother's masks have watched over me and my eBay business. I've got to get them back on a wall!

# #7  Pinheiro Cat Tile

$1.00
**Paid**
**From:** Estate sale

**Portugal Majolica Tile Kitty Cat Bordallo Pinheiro NEAT**

**Description:**
Ceramic majolica tile. This is an awesome piece. Kitty cat face with cabbage leaves and a collar and bells. 5⅜" square and in excellent condition. Signed "Portugal Bordallo Pinheiro."

**Winning Bid:**

# $47.55

**Ended:** 6/09/05
**History:** 19 bids
**Starting Bid:** $9.99
**Winner:** Alpharetta, GA

**Viewed**
000145 X

## The Story

My mom and I were at an estate sale and the moment we walked in, I knew I should start making piles. Prices were reasonable and this person had been a collector of items from all over the world.

I started grabbing cats, elephants and dinnerware and I put them on a shelf that I labeled as mine. My mom and I took turns guarding it. This cat tile was one of those items.

Signed tiles are usually quite collectible, and the signature on this one looked like "Bordallo Pinheiro" and "Portugal." I listed it without researching the company at all. I don't do much research anymore, and typically only research individual items when I'm writing a book. Isn't that weird?

When I started out on eBay back in 1998, I would spend hours on research. I have come to realize that those were wasted hours—hours that I could have spent listing more items and making more money. This book is not long enough to explain the Dralle Method in more detail, but maximizing selling volume is a cornerstone of my business (to learn more, take a look at www.bootcampbox.com ).

Now that this tile has sold and provided me with a great return on my $1 investment, I decided to include it in this book and finally do some research. Yipppeeee!

It turns out that the most famous and successful of any Portuguese ceramist is virtually unknown in the US. His name was Rafael Augusto Bardalo Pinheiro, and he lived from 1846 to 1905. He was an incredible artist who also designed more commercial ceramic tiles.

After his death in 1905, Rafael's company eventually closed, but in 1922, a group of businessmen built a new factory on the same site, which today employs 350 workers. It exports 80% of its wares, largely to the U.S.

Many of the original Rafael tiles are still reproduced today, and it turns out that this was what I had—a newer, reproduced tile from a Rafael Bordalo Pinheiro original design. And what a neat tile it was—a cat's head with a cabbage leaf background. As you can see in my title, I thought that the tile was majolica, but this company claims it is faience. Let's take a look at the difference.

Faience is traditionally French, as its name suggests. It is tin-glazed earthenware with an opaque glaze and a highly colorful decoration, often with a strong greenish blue.

Majolica is traditionally Italian and Spanish. It is pottery glazed with tin enamel and usually decorated with bright, festive colors. The general term "majolica" is also used to describe any pottery with an opaque tin enamel glaze that conceals the color of the clay body. This would include delft, faience and the more familiar majolica of England, Spain, Germany, Italy and the U.S.

So "majolica" is the broad term, and "faience" is a type of majolica. So I was correct in calling this tile "majolica," and more importantly, my $1 investment turned into almost $50 with no research! No research makes my eBay world spin around faster and faster.

# #8 Tchaikovsky Butterfly Plate

**$0.50** Paid
**From:** Charity sale

## England English Tchaikovsky Brass Butterfly Plate OLD!

**Description:**
Vintage plate is 6". Signed "England," brass Tchaikovsky plate with butterfly border. Copper center and brass butterflies on the edge. The glass cover over the composer's head needs cleaning. Otherwise in great condition.

**Winning Bid:** **$32.<sup>73</sup>**

**Ended:** 6/16/05
**History:** 6 bids
**Starting Bid:** $9.99
**Winner:** Pasadena, CA

**Viewed**
000029 X

# Tchaikovsky Butterfly Plate #8

## The Story

You see these composer plates EVERYWHERE. I am not kidding. I run across at least one of them every month. They are typically priced very cheaply—anywhere from ten cents to $1 each. I always pick them up, and I can usually get $9.99 for them.

I wanted to write about this plate because I had never had one sell for so much money before. Over $30 for a common item like this is unheard of. So I wanted to figure out why Tchaikovsky's plate brought in more money than any of the others. The history I found on his life was fascinating.

He was born in Russia in 1840 and began piano lessons at the age of five. When his mother died of cholera in 1854, the fourteen-year-old composed a waltz in her memory.

My parents made me take piano lessons starting at the age of ten. I hated it. My torment lasted for just four short years, but it was enough to scar me for life. Not really. But I am totally NOT musically inclined, and the lessons were painful. One of the reasons that I hated them so much was that my parents often forgot to pick me up.

I would wait in the pouring rain and no one would show up to get me. I didn't want to go back into the piano teacher's house, so I would tough it out on the curb. This was in the day of no cell phones (imagine that), and in cold, wet weather, a half hour felt like a lifetime. I think this is the reason that I am NEVER late picking up my kids. Making sure that they never have to wait like I did is important to me.

I also think that the memory of those awful lessons is the reason I don't own a piano and have not had my kids take any type of music lessons. I need to rethink this, because my daughter Indiana is extremely talented musically. She even sings in the Desert Chorale Children's Choir (a huge honor).

But back to Tchaikovsky. His life was filled with nervous breakdowns and suicide attempts, yet despite the turmoil in his life, he wrote amazing music. He is responsible for the scores to Swan Lake, Sleeping Beauty and The Nutcracker. Isn't that awesome?

The most influential woman in Tchaikovsky's life was a wealthy widow named Nadezhda von Meck, with whom he exchanged over 1,200 letters. Can you imagine what one of those would sell for on eBay? (My mind is always in the eBay gutter.)

At Nadezhda's insistence, the pair never met; they did run into each other twice by accident, but did not talk. She backed him financially to the tune of 6,000 rubles a year; after thirteen years, she ended the relationship.

By the time Nadezhda's sponsorship ended, Tchaikovsky had become very successful in Europe and was receiving even greater accolades in the U.S. In fact, he was the conductor at the official opening night of Carnegie Hall. How cool is that?

What an interesting, tormented artist. I can now understand why this plate sold for so much more than others. I can't be called a tormented artist—just a kid whose parents forgot to pick her up. Oh, well—not much tragedy here.

# #9  RS Prussia Vase

$10.00
**Paid**
**From:** Estate sale

**RS Prussia Germany Royal Preussen Antique Vase Dog RARE**

## Description:

RS Prussia vase is very amazing and beautiful. Signed "Germany Royal Preussen," 14⅜" by 6½". I was told that "Preussen" means Prussia. In the same family as RS Prussia but I could not find out anything else about this company. If anyone knows, please fill us in. Two handles and wonderful art nouveau style. 1890s I am guessing. There is a woman with a dog on the front. Looks like some type of hound, shepherd or hunting dog. The colors and detail are exquisite. Blue, purple, yellow etc. It has been repaired at the rim and this repair job could definitely be improved upon. I have shown the repair from two angles. It is about 2" by 1". There is also a small repair at the back base, ¾" by ¼". This vase is being sold as is but with some expert repair work, it could be a masterpiece.

**Winning Bid:** $501.99

**Ended:** 6/18/05
**History:** 11 bids
**Starting Bid:** $24.99
**Winner:** Fairmont, NC

**Viewed**
000532 X

# RS Prussia Vase   #9

## The Story

I have used the same publicist over the years. Her name is Meg McCallister and she is awesome! Unfortunately, publicity for my eBay books has been tough to come by. Most of the media do not want to give eBay free advertising. They want eBay to spend from their deep pockets and purchase publicity.

Oh, well. You live and learn. I will tell you one thing that Meg did for me that changed my eBay business in an incredible way. She talked me into exhibiting at eBay Live that I had avoided because I assumed it was a real cutthroat type of event—not my idea of fun.

But after discussing it with Meg, I decided to go for it (thank you, Meg!). We were able to squeeze into eBay Live in June of 2005. Two weeks before the event, while Mo and I were packing up product and strategizing our booth layout for eBay Live, my mom and I went out garage saling.

On this particular Saturday, we ended up in a section of Palm Desert that is super close to my house and is known as the "State Streets." We rarely go in to that area because we never find anything. Well, this was all about to change.

It was an estate sale that had advertised "lots of antiques." On the ground in front of a shelf I found this vase. It was beautiful. A real old-time antique, and even though it was in as-is condition, the sellers still wanted $10 for it. I put it in my pile, but hadn't really made up my mind about it.

I bought a lot of items that day, and while deciding about this vase, it dawned on me that it was a piece that my grandmother would have loved. It was just the type of vase that she and the other old-time dealers

would have featured in their stores or in their booths at antiques shows. I decided to go for it. "The last of the big time spenders," I could just hear my grandmother saying to me—another of her favorite sayings.

When I got home and did my research (Okay, Okay, I still do a little bit of research—I can't help myself!), I found that the signature "Preussen" means "Prussia," which was a kingdom in north-central Europe that includes present-day northern Germany and northern Poland. Although this piece wasn't signed "RS Prussia," it was done in the same style as an RS Prussia piece and seemed to be from the same region.

RS (Reinhold Schlegelmilch) Prussia is very, very collectible. An RS Prussia vase similar to my purchase but in excellent condition had recently sold for $220. I was hoping for $100 for my vase, so I started the bidding at $24.99 (to cover my $10 investment).

I was shocked and extremely excited when this vase sold for over $500. The buyer paid with a money order, which made me think that he or she was an old-time collector. I hope that the vase was professionally repaired, because it was an amazing piece and helped to pay for my booth at eBay Live. I need a new bumper sticker: "Will trade antiques for booth space."

# #10  Pfaltzgraff Sauce Dish

**$3.<sup>00</sup>**
Paid
**From:** Estate sale

## American Bone China Pfaltzgraff Yuletide Sauce Bowl WOW

**Description:**
This Pfaltzgraff yuletide porcelain sauce bowl was made in America. It is a very hard to find and rare pattern since Pfaltzgraff typically just manufacturers stoneware.   The bowl is 5⅛" in diameter and could be  used for sauce, dessert or fruit.  In excellent condition. Lovely pattern.

**Winning Bid:**

**$52.<sup>51</sup>**

**Ended:** 6/22/05
**History:** 12 bids
**Starting Bid:** $9.99
**Winner:** Suffield, CT

**Viewed**
`000065` X

# Pfaltzgraff Sauce Dish   #10

## The Story

Well, fresh off of my RS Prussia vase high, Mo and I packed my car and took off for eBay Live. While Mo and I were on our way to San Jose—(hey, isn't that a song?)— this piece sold for an incredible amount of money.

I found this tiny sauce bowl at the estate sale in the state streets where I picked up the $500 vase. It was marked $3, and it was Pfaltzgraff. I have never had good luck with Pfaltzgraff and can spot it from a mile away, and when I do I usually run. For some reason, this bowl tickled my fancy (another saying I picked up from Cheryl Leaf). It was bone china, which I hadn't realized Pfaltzgraff made. I had only seen their stoneware.

So, you can imagine my surprise when I looked up the pattern on Replacements and saw that one dinner plate sells for $99.95. Yippee! Replacements also had zero sauce dishes in stock and no published price. Another great sign. A sauce dish is a small bowl that can be used for dessert, fruit, or actual sauces. When I list one of these, I try to put all three uses in the title (if there is room).

Oddly enough, my grandmother collected sauce dishes. Well, maybe not so odd, because she collected almost everything! The sauce dishes she collected were EAPG (Early American Pattern Glass) and done in the most beautiful colors.

I remember that she would use them on the table with different sauces (ketchup, cranberry sauce and so on). My grandmother always said, "What is the point of owning beautiful things if you can't enjoy them?" She used all her valuables. They were never stored in a bank vault where no one could appreciate them.

So back to our drive up to San Jose for eBay Live. Mo and I were talking so much that we missed the turn off for I-5 and ended up driving through Bakersfield. I called my brother and said, "I don't think we are on the right road." He often answers his phone with a deadpan, "OnStar" when he knows I am calling for directions. Anyway, he laughed at us when we all finally realized that we had accidentally taken I-90 and were now two hours out of our way. The big joke became, "Do you know the way to San Jose?" Obviously not!

We finally made it to the convention center, and as we stepped out of the car I was immediately interviewed for local TV. You see, our detour paid off! eBay Live was a blast. We met a ton of incredible eBayers, authors, and just plain characters. Mo and I had the time of our lives. We sold a lot of product, made new friends, and I even got to dance to the B-52's with Griff (Dean of eBay Education). It doesn't get better than this—except when you can sell one Pfaltzgraff sauce dish for over $50!

Do you know the way to San José?

# #11  2 Japanese Cloisonné Vases

$10.⁰⁰/2
Paid
From: Garage sale

**Japanese Antique Cloisonné Enamel Vase Bird Yellow WOW!**

## Description:

Japanese Antique vase is 7¼" by 4". Yellow base with lovely floral flowering flower design. This vase even has a bird on one of the branches. I think that yellow is a rare color as you hardly ever see it in the antique Japanese work. Usually the colors are darker. The flowers are pink and white and could be tiger lilies or calla lilies (lilly). They are wonderfully done and shaded. The work is very fine as is typical for Japanese cloisonné. Also, very typical for Japanese cloisonné is to leave a lot of empty space. This vase has the design on the front and yellow all around. Silver wires and silver metal top and base. It has a dark green enamel inside. I would guess 1880s to 1920s. Definitely antique.

Winning Bid: **$158.⁵⁶/2**

**Ended:** 6/26/05
**History:** 11 bids on 2
**Starting Bid:** $24.99 each
**Winners:** Burns, TN
Essex, UK

Viewed
000292 X

# 2 Japanese Cloisonné Vases  #11

## The Story

In April, Maureen and I had exhibited at the LA Times Festival of Books. It wasn't really my target market and the show was not very successful for us. Too many highbrow intellectual types. My McGraw Hill antiques book was just out, however, and the festival had promised me a book signing. Well, the day before the festival began, my McGraw Hill publicist called to say that the signing got cancelled. Bummer!

So to make up for it, they were going to schedule a book signing at Borders in Rancho Mirage. OK—my first book signing at a major bookstore. Pretty exciting. However, they scheduled me for June 30th—dead of summer—120 degrees. Probably not a whole lot of people would be in our area. But I was positive and excited about it and began preparing.

My mom and I had been to another garage sale in the state streets. From the car, I spotted a pair of yellow lamps that were quite lovely. The lady wanted $10 and I had a funny feeling about them. They were something more than porcelain—they almost felt like enamel.

Well, I got them home and took a closer look and was thrilled to find out that they were Japanese cloisonné. Cloisonné produced in Japan is high quality. In addition, these pieces were originally vases that had been made into lamps. Wow! Back in the 1940s, that was all the rage. People got crazy and started drilling holes in beautiful vases to make them into lamps. Watch

for these. They will typically sell much better when turned back into vases.

What was also interesting was that they didn't match exactly. One had a bird on it and the other didn't. My dad was visiting and I had him take the lamps apart so that I could sell them as vases.

Since I had these amazing examples of Japanese cloisonné, I decided to bring them with me to feature at my book signing along with a really neat sample of how cloisonné is made.

So there I was at my book signing, with all these great teaching tools. How many people showed up, not including my family? A total of two! How embarrassing, and no one even bought a book.

Fortunately, my dad, Houston, Indiana and my mom were there to relieve my embarrassment and feel my pain. Also, Indy's good friend Paige was there. Indy had met Paige on her first day of pre-school and had decided then and there that Paige was going to be her best friend. Paige wanted nothing to do with her. But my daughter's perseverance paid off, and I am happy to say that they are still best friends after four years—from age four to eight! Those are important formative years!

Where would I be without my friends and family? I am very grateful to all of them! And those two vases ended up selling for over $150! That eased my embarrassment slightly. No more book signings!

# #12  Flapper Head

**$0.⁰⁰**

Paid

**From:** Inheritance

**Porcelain 1/2 Half Face Head Doll Flapper Antique RARE**

## Description:

Porcelain half doll is a fun piece. I would guess the 1920s. I have never seen another one like it. It is 2⅛" by 1¼" by ⅞". Looks to be a flapper with a black hat, brown curls and blue eyes. It is marked or stamped 1619. Four little holes to sew onto something. It was originally sewn on velvet and framed when I found it in my grandmother's antique collection of dolls. In very good condition.

**Winning
Bid:**

**$61.⁰⁰**

**Ended:** 6/28/05
**History:** 5 bids
**Starting Bid:** $9.99
**Winner:** NSW Australia

**Viewed**

000077 X

# Flapper Head #12

## The Story

One of my grandmother's collections was half-dolls. Half-dolls are generally the upper half of a human figure—so no legs. They were made to be attached to something like a pin cushion, whisk broom or tea cozy. Half-dolls were a feminine accessory, and date back to the days when a lady would have enjoyed afternoon tea in her "boudoir."

The vast majority of half-dolls were made between 1900 and 1920. The more complex the mold, the higher the value. Those with arms close to the body are generally the least expensive, because only a simple two-part mold would have been required to make them. Those with openings between the arms and body are the next most valuable, and those with arms that don't touch the body are most valuable of all.

The rarest half-dolls are those that are holding trays with pots of hot chocolate and cups. This type of half-doll is called "La Belle Chocolatier" (beautiful chocolate girl). The history of the chocolate girl is very interesting. In 1745, Prince Dietrichstein of Austria stopped at a chocolate shop in Vienna to see if this new drink, hot chocolate, was as wonderful as everyone claimed. The waitress who served him was a beautiful young lady, Anna Baltrauf, the daughter of a poor knight.

In spite of strong objections, Anna and the prince were soon married. As a wedding gift, her portrait was painted with her serving chocolate in a 17th-century costume. For more than 100 years the portrait hung in the Dresden Art Gallery in Germany. In 1862, the president of Walter Baker Chocolates visited and admired the painting.

He thought it would be a wonderful trademark for his company, and the image of "La Belle Chocolatier" is still used by Baker's chocolates today. Keep your eyes peeled for "La Belle Chocolatier" half-dolls. They are worth bucks!

Most half-dolls are unmarked, but some have a four- or five-digit style number and maybe a country of origin. Look for half-dolls made in Germany and France: they are quite rare and valuable.

My grandmother's half-doll was not your typical half-doll, although it did have the four-digit style mark typical of older German pieces.

I called the face a flapper, but it may also have been intended as a Pierrot. We listed this for sale on eBay back when my grandmother was alive and we still had the antique shop. It sold for only $15, and for some reason the buyer was not pleased with it and wanted to return it. Fine. I never want an unhappy customer.

Fast forward to 2005 and I found this half-doll in one of the boxes I inherited. I thought I would give it a whirl on eBay again. Well, this time it sold for a much more respectable price. I shipped it to Australia and it stuck. I mean that the customer was happy and the sale was final!

I wonder if my grandmother ever took her afternoon tea in her boudoir. Somehow I doubt it, but I do know this. My grandmother would be much happier knowing that her half doll sold for over $60 instead of just $15. Sometimes a return can have a silver lining!

# #13 Spode 'The Hunt' Dinner Set

$400.<sup>00</sup>/38

Paid

**From:** Estate sale

**Cache Pot Cachepot The Hunt Meet Vintage Spode Horses**

**Description:**
This is a cache pot cachepot in "The Hunt" pattern by Spode. Design is "The Meet." Use as a planter. 6½" tall. In excellent condition. Needs cleaning. No chips, cracks or crazing. We have a lot of pieces in this pattern for sale this week. It is a great pattern by Spode and was designed by the artist Herring. Pattern is called "The Hunt" and is of horses and hunters. Pattern # 2/9265. Discontinued and only made from 1948 to 1995. Camilla shape, green outer band.

**Winning Bid:** $1706.<sup>31</sup>/38

**Ended:** 7/9/05
**History:** 371 bids/38 pieces
**Starting Bids:** $9.99 to $24.99
**Winners:** MA, NJ, OK

**Viewed**
001282 X

# Spode 'The Hunt' Dinner Set #13

## The Story

I hear from many of my ezine subscribers (visit TheQueenofAuctions. com for free signup) that they don't know what to do for merchandise in the off season—typically the winter. It is funny, because out here in Palm Desert our off season is during the summer! When it is 120 degrees, there isn't much going on!

My advice is to stock up during the regular garage sale season and hit your thrift stores during the off season. Keep your eyes open for estate sales all year.

Even if there is just one sale in your newspaper that Saturday—it can really pay off to attend. I found this out in July of 2005 when my mom and I headed over to Palm Springs for the only estate sale listed in the paper. Wow! What a bonanza. The house had at one time belonged to Bette Davis—or so legend has it. It was located in the Movie Star Colony and this family had impeccable taste and tons of dishes.

It was the last day of the sale and the seller was ready to deal. He let me buy this 49-piece Spode set for half price (a $400 savings), a Royal Albert Old Country Roses set for half price (a $475 savings) and an entire table full of silverplate for $100. It was quite the exciting purchase! I get such a rush out of buying in bulk.

It is funny, but I don't like shopping at all. I hate going to the mall, or spending anytime walking down our expensive shopping areas here in Palm Desert. But put me at a good estate sale and I will shop till I drop! I think that I was cured of shopping when I was a buyer for the May Company department stores and I had to shop for a living.

Anyway, this Spode pattern was incredible. The Spode company was founded around 1770 by Josiah Spode I. In 1805, W.T. Copeland became a partner with Josiah Spode II and in 1812 took over the Spode company completely. The Spode name was used alongside the Copeland name throughout the 19th and 20th centuries. In 1970, to honor the founder, the name reverted to Spode. Keep this in mind when dating Spode pieces.

The pattern I had was called "The Hunt" and featured horses and their riders at different stages of a fox hunt. Many of the scenes were derived from drawings and paintings by an artist named J.F. Herring. Herring was born in 1795 and made a living of sorts painting inn signs, coach panels, and portraits of horses.

By 1830, he was heavily in debt, and W.T. Copeland took over his bills and invited him to live in a house on his estate in Essex. Copeland commissioned Herring to paint pictures of his racehorses, fox hunts, and other aspects of rural life. It is from these paintings that most of the scenes for "The Hunt" are derived. "The Hunt" was first introduced in 1930 and discontinued in the mid-1990s.

I broke the 49 pieces of Spode "The Hunt" out into 38 auctions. The piece that sold for the most was the cache pot for $117.75. My pieces were post-1970 since they did not also include Copeland in the signature. My $400 investment turned into over $1700 during that hot, hot summer month!

# #14 Blue Onion Tureen

**$10.00**
Paid
**From:** Thrift store

## Blue Onion Flow Blue Tureen 4 Pc Vintage Meissen Style

### Description:

Blue Onion Tureen is a great four-piece set. Vintage or antique. Says "Blue Onion" and has crossed arrows on the base. No country of manufacture. I would guess 1940s to 1950s. Double tureen with a lid, ladle, body and underplate (the four pieces). Flow blue style. 19¾" by 10". Needs cleaning. One tiny ⅛" round nick on the base of the tureen.

**Winning Bid:**

**$79.00**

**Ended:** 7/17/05
**History:** 17 bids
**Starting Bid:** $9.99
**Winner:** Arcadia, CA

Viewed
000165 X

# Blue Onion Tureen   #14

## The Story

It was hot, hot, hot here in the desert. My kids were in Bellingham for several weeks with their grandpa (my dad), so Peter and I decided to go to Cabo San Lucas for a few days to scuba dive. It's still hot there, but at least I would be getting away to the ocean and would be in a beautiful city.

Right before my mini-trip, I found this tureen in my local thrift store. It was priced at $20, which is quite high for a garage sale, but not so high anymore for a thrift store. As many of us have noticed, the thrift stores are out of control with their pricing. They think that they are high-end retailing establishments where people will pay top dollar. Think again!

Many thrift stores are even printing out the Replacements.com pricing information and putting it next to their dishware. Give me a break! They will lose their biggest customer base—us dealers—if they keep this up.

Some of these thrift stores are setting the prices so high that items sit on the shelves for months on end. I can only seriously shop when they have their half-price sales. Luckily for me, that July they were having a half-price sale and I was able to get the tureen for $10.

As many of you may have noticed, my self-imposed $5 limit is not in effect anymore. I will spend more than $5 for higher quality items, which is exactly what I did that day in July.

By the way, the $5 limit is very helpful when you are first starting out on eBay. Even with my antiques background, the $5 limit has saved me more times than I care to mention. It has

just been in the last several years that I have started investing more money as I feel that I have learned the eBay ropes—so to speak.

I knew that the pattern on the tureen was famous, and fortunately for me its name was written on the base: Blue Onion. Blue Onion was originally produced by Meissen China from 1720 to 1739. The pattern itself is not an onion at all; it's a pomegranate that slightly resembles the outline of an onion.

The design is a grouping of peaches and the pomegranate with stylized peonies and asters in the center, the stems of which wind in flowing curves around a bamboo stalk. The pattern appears to be symmetrical, but if you look closely you can see that it is actually asymmetrical, and has a highly ornamental Rococo feel. Based on the plant types it depicts, experts say Blue Onion probably has its roots in an Asian pattern that was copied by the German Meissen factory in the 18th century. Wherever it came from, the Blue Onion design has had a permanency over the years, and it still has a widespread appeal today.

Many companies have produced variations of this Blue Onion pattern over the years, and my piece was not a true Meissen piece. However, there is still a huge following for the blue and white "Zwiebelmuster" ("onion pattern" in German) design to this day.

So while Peter and I were having lobster bisque at Lorenzillos in Cabo San Lucas, this darling piece sold for almost $80—more than enough to pay for our soup.

# #15  Arthur Court Rabbit Tray

**$1.**<sup></sup>**00**
Paid
From: Garage sale

## Arthur Court MIB Bunny Rabbit Plate Cheese Server 2001

**Description:**
This neat Arthur Court mint in box cheese server is from 2001. Looks like it has never been used. There is an aluminum serving tray and a cheese server/knife/spreader. Box is 10" by 8½". Style number is 04-0676. Features a bunny rabbit.

**Winning Bid:**

**$32.**<sup></sup>**00**
**Ended:** 7/17/05
**History:** 15 bids
**Starting Bid:** $9.99
**Winner:** Edmund, OK

**Viewed**
000098 X

# Arthur Court Rabbit Tray #15

## The Story

I was deep into writing the Wiley *Unofficial Guide to Making Money on eBay.* The day after I had returned from Cabo, a third of the manuscript was due. Talk about pressure—about 123 pages of serious text. We are not talking the fun text that you find in these *100 Best Books,* but the serious text of a how-to manual.

I had never considered writing a how-to book, but to have credibility in the eBay teaching world, I needed to write a serious how-to book and have it published by one of the majors.

There are literally thousands of book publishers in the United States, but McGraw-Hill and John Wiley are among the top ten in market share.

So I bit the bullet and went for it. My dad, mom, friends and family helped with my kids for most of that summer so I could write and still sell on eBay. They are all awesome! And while all this was happening, I found this darling bunny rabbit tray at a garage sale for $1. It was mint in the original box and made by Arthur Court. I have always had good luck with Arthur Court items.

Arthur and Elena Court are the founders of the company. Arthur was raised on a farm in Minnesota and spent eighteen years working for design and decorating firms in San Francisco. He was very involved with mineral collecting and traveled the globe looking for exotic specimens for his company Arthur Court Design, founded in 1966. He is best known for intricate and wonderful aluminum creations that make up the majority of the company's business today.

Elena Orsini-Court is a native San Franciscan. She studied oriental art history and modern art and was a curator for public art exhibitions. Currently, she is director of product development and president of Arthur Court design.

What really struck me about the Courts and their company is their passion to give back to society with both their time and money. A portion of all sales of their products funds wildlife preservation and protection as well as environmental research and education. They often use nature as the inspiration for their products and the Arthur Court aluminum bunnies are very collectible.

What I had was one of the bunnies. Cool! The lady that bought it purchased it as a gift for a dear friend who collects rabbits, specifically Arthur Court Bunnies. The ironic part of the story is that Cyndy, the buyer, still has not given the tray to her good friend and it sits in a little stash in her closet.

Don't we all have stashes in our closets? Gifts that we have purchased for our friends and families that we put away to be given later? I have an entire closet devoted to gifts that I have collected all year in anticipation of the perfect occasion that will be coming soon.

The day that I finished the Wiley book would be the perfect occasion to have a party—and the perfect excuse to break out some of those gifts to give back a little to my friends and family that supported me that entire summer. All through the long, hard, and tedious process of writing a book for a major publisher!

# #16 Huge Brass Scale

**$138.68 Paid**

From: eBay Reseller pallet

## Huge Gumps Brass Scale Decorator's Dream Awesome! MIB

### Description:
Huge Gumps Brass Scale comes mint in the original box. This is an amazing large brass scale for decoration only. It is so awesome! 42" tall by 38" by 13¼". It will be the focal point of any room. In excellent condition. The box had never been opened until we put it together for the photos. I have lots and lots of new in box gift items up for sale from world famous Gumps (San Francisco). These are all very high quality items and all have never been used. Please check all of our auctions for more wonderful things from Gumps.

**Winning Bid:** **$299.00**

**Ended:** 7/24/05
**History:** 8 bids
**Starting Bid:** $49.99, $299 reserve
**Winner:** Baton Rouge, LA

**Viewed**
000152 X

## The Story

I love this story! At eBay Live in San Jose, I stumbled upon the Power Seller's Lounge and once inside (after grabbing several free Diet Cokes) I saw a booth for the Reseller Marketplace.

It looked extremely interesting and I went over to learn more. The eBay Reseller Marketplace is a special auction site set up for PowerSellers only. PowerSellers (like me and hopefully you) can bid on and purchase huge or small lots of items from manufacturers, jobbers, wholesalers and other approved sellers. Then we can resell the items on eBay. It sounded really cool. As soon as I got home from eBay Live, I placed bids on four different auctions.

I ended up winning a 56-piece lot for $1,607 and all the items were from Gumps of San Francisco, which is a very high end retailer. I love Gumps.

I ended up paying about 23 cents on the dollar, and one of the items was a huge brass decorator's scale. Original retail was $600, and I paid $138.68. I thought that if I could double my money that would be great.

So I listed the scale with a $49.99 starting bid price and a $299.00 reserve. Well, lo and behold, that scale ended up selling for the reserve price! The story gets even better because of where it ended up—in the home of a school teacher named Marcy in Baton Rouge, LA.

Here is what she emailed me:

I was a teacher for 23 years and recently retired. At the end of every school year, the parents give the teachers a gift certificate. I had been watching a designer's scale on the Gump's website but it was way too expensive for me to purchase, so I had planned to use the gift certificate to pay for it. I watched that catalog site every month all year and there was that scale. Still there...waiting for me!!

School ended and I rushed home that day to get MY scale. It was gone. I called the store in California and learned it had been discontinued and none were left. I was SOOO crushed. I had watched that doggone scale for almost a year. I didn't even think about eBay at that point.

Then one day I was thinking about my scale and I just typed in "scale" on the eBay search page and lo and behold...MY SCALE was there! There was no doubt that this scale would now be mine. My husband had been hearing about it for over a year and he said to get it no matter what the price.

(Lynn speaking here, "Darn it! I should have gone for full retail." Just kidding!)

Well, I won the bid! Yeah!! But the scale was far too large for our home and we had no place to put it. We also owned an eighteen-foot-long table that came from a library in Scotland, and we had no place for it either.

We eventually remodeled our home and added a very long loggia (sunroom) to the front of the house. The table fit perfectly in this room and the scale went onto the table. It looks absolutely grand! I LOVE the scale.

What a great story. 'Nuff said.

# #17  Arabia Vase

$5.00
**Paid**
**From:** Thrift store

**Alice Arabia Finland Sunflower Vase Hilkka Liisa Ahola**

### Description:

Arabia sunflower vase is very neat. Signed "HLA" for Hilkka-Liisa Ahola, one of the resident artists for Arabia from 1947 to 1974. I would guess that this piece is 1960s. Signed also with "Alice Arabia Finland HLA NS." Could be a vase or utensil holder. 6" by 4¼" and in excellent condition. Similar to the sun rose pattern. I believe the pattern is "Alice."

WE WILL BE ON VACATION FROM AUGUST 18TH TO AUGUST 25TH, SO THERE WILL BE NO SHIPPING DURING THAT TIME PERIOD. IF THIS IS A PROBLEM, PLEASE DO NOT BID. THANKS!

**Winning Bid:**

**$56.00**

**Ended:** 8/26/05
**History:** 8 bids
**Starting Bid:** $9.99
**Winner:** Minneapolis, MN

**Viewed**
000087 X

# Arabia Vase #17

## The Story

For the first time ever in my Southern California eBay career, I would be without an assistant for the summer. Oh no! Mo (Maureen) typically spent every summer in Minnesota and Canada. I couldn't blame her—the temperatures here in the hot months are really unbearable.

It was a long summer but I was muddling through without her. The pallets from eBay Live helped, because all the items were already packed and ready to ship. Also, my sister came down for several weeks to help and my mom was also a lifesaver.

But it turned out that there was one week that both Mo and I were going to be gone. I would be spending three weeks in Bellingham, and she wouldn't be returning until about ten days after we headed north.

So in every listing I put the large warning you see in my description. Back then, eBay didn't have the feature that allows you to actually put your eBay store on vacation. How cool is that new option? eBay is always thinking!

So while I was in Bellingham doing another book signing, this neat vase was up for sale. Didn't I swear off book signings in a recent story? Well, let me explain. There is an awesome book store in the Fairhaven area of Bellingham called Village Books. I grew up shopping there when they were first starting out and still very tiny. Now they are a recognized leader in the independent book store world.

I had been asking them for a signing but it didn't seem to float until I ran into Village Book owners Chuck and Dee Robinson at Book Expo in New York. They were impressed that I was writing the Wiley book and asked me to please email their coordinator to set up a date. How exciting! My only worry was that only two people would show up—like in Rancho Mirage—and those two people would be related to me. At least I have a lot of family in Bellingham—maybe four people would show.

So my brother and I sent out a postcard mailing to the old Cheryl Leaf Antiques mailing list and then crossed our fingers! The signing was held on a Wednesday night at 7:30 pm in August. I showed up (nervous as all get out) and couldn't believe that Village Books had to keep adding chairs.

It wasn't really a book signing so much as a book discussion. I actually had to speak for over an hour. There were more than 100 people there: some customers from the shop, some aunts and uncles, my kids, and so many of my friends! It was awesome!

Back to my thrift store find that was selling for a lot! I always pick up Arabia Finland items whenever I see them. This one had the artist's initials on the base. Her name was Hilkka-Liisa Ahola; she worked for Arabia from 1947 to 1974, and she was famous for her sunflowers.

My mortifying first book signing had now been replaced with a much sunnier (sunflower) memory, and this neat vase that I bought for $5 sold for over $50! "I can't complain," as my grandmother would have said! She was definitely with me in spirit that night in Bellingham.

# #18   Red Hot Lips Telephone

$0.⁵⁰ **Paid**
**From:** Garage sale

**Red Hot Lips Lipstick Vintage Telephone Telequest RETRO**

### Description:
Red hot lips telephone is so cute. 8" by 4" by 2½". RETRO. Needs cleaning but does work. Telequest 1984. Needs both cords—the one to connect the two pieces and the one for the wall. There are some really tiny crazing lines in the plastic. Still really neat.

**Winning Bid:**

$14.¹⁹
**Ended:** 8/29/05
**History:** 2 bids
**Starting Bid:** $9.99
**Winner:** Italy

**Viewed**

000053 X

# Red Hot Lips Telephone   #18

## The Story

This darling phone was from 1984. It got me to wondering, "Where was I in 1984?" The answer is "Spain." I was spending part of my junior year at USC's Madrid campus. How cool was that? My grandmother did a lot to help make so many of my wonderful adventures happen.

My brother was also in Spain for his senior year of high school—so for spring break, my grandmother brought the entire cast and crew over to spend Easter week in Italy. What a great time we had! We visited the leaning tower of Pisa, Capri (my favorite), Florence, Venice (amazing), and Naples.

Traveling with my grandmother gave me some of my favorite memories. She lived for travel, and it was very hard for her in the last eight years of her life when travel wasn't an option. She always wanted to go to Australia, but it was one country she never visited. I am determined to see it for her.

But in the summer of 2005, I was traveling in eastern Washington for our annual high school girls' weekend. We were at Karen Bass's home in Wenatchee, and Cashmere was the next town over. My grandmother grew up in Cashmere, so going there was always bittersweet.

I asked my good friend Jo Dallas if she would drive me over as she had done two years earlier. Of course. This time, the lady who lived in my grandmother's childhood home was there when Jo and I knocked on the door to ask if we could take a look. I was shaking—it was very emotional.

She was kind enough to let us in, so I got to see the bedrooms, the living room, the famous sleeping porch, and the steep staircase that lead to the upstairs bedrooms. I knew that my grandmother's bedroom was one of those upstairs, because she always told the story of how her stepmother would call in a lilting voice up the staircase, "Cheryl, are your lights out?" and my grandma would say "Yes, mother" as she pulled the cord. My grandmother loved to read, and she would leave her lights on as long as she could without lying.

It was a very poignant visit for me, and afterward I needed a distraction. As Jo and I were leaving, we spotted a sign for a garage sale close to the church in which my grandmother had been married. Jo is always a trooper and drove straight to the sale, where I found this phone for 50 cents.

Then we headed toward Lake Chelan. A big part of this girls' weekend was spending a day on the lake. The weather was beautiful, and I ended up conquering my fear enough to actually go tubing. Even though I was terrified at times, I spent most of the time laughing really hard!

Seeing the inside of my grandmother's childhood home reminded me of how much I still miss her, and a totally carefree day on the lake helped me to feel a little less emotional.

This vintage phone sold for $14.19 and the winning bidder paid $15 (more than the cost of the phone) to have it shipped airmail to Italy. How strange that Italy was where I was during spring break of the year it was made—1984—and now the phone lives (and hopefully rings) in Italy!

# #19 Eames Era Metal Ring

$0.⁰⁰ **Paid**

**From:** Inheritance

## Silver Metal Ring Eames Era Mid Century Modern COOL!

### Description:

Silver metal ring is so cool! Costume ring is silver metal. This ring is approximately a 7.5 but is adjustable. What a neat piece of 1950s art to wear or display. The top part is ⅞" by ⅞". The shank is a little bent but in overall great condition. My brother, who is GIA (Gemological Institute of America) certified has checked and helped identify this piece. We have a lot of awesome jewelry up for sale this week.

**Winning Bid:** $35.⁶⁷

**Ended:** 9/2/05
**History:** 5 bids
**Starting Bid:** $9.99
**Winner:** Matawan, NJ

**Viewed**
000113 X

# Eames Era Metal Ring #19

## The Story

My grandmother was sooo talented. She not only made jewelry by stringing beads together, but she actually created pieces using lost wax casting. What in the heck is lost wax casting anyway? I don't really know, but you had better believe that I am going to find out for this story.

I remember my grandmother always taking classes at museums, the local community college, or wherever she could find them. She had a thirst for knowledge and there was nothing she enjoyed more than learning with others. I can remember fellow students from her lost wax class coming into the shop to show my grandmother what they had made. It was pretty cool.

There were always sheets of red wax, sand, and plaster molds around her jewelry area. I never really understood how the lost wax process worked, and now is a great time to figure it out.

Well, lost wax casting is an ancient practice that is still used today. It involves over fifteen steps, so we can't discuss them all. But basically, the artist first creates an original piece of art from wax, then creates a plaster mold around it. The wax is then melted out of the plaster.

Once the plaster mold is finished, molten metal is poured into it. The cooling metal takes on the shape of the "lost" wax sculpture, which has literally disappeared—hence the name.

My grandmother often looked to her antique collections for inspiration. She would use some of her three-dimensional antique jasper plaques in her lost wax work, pouring plaster over them to make the mold, then creating the wax duplicate from that. Last week, my mom brought over one of my grandmother's favorite plaster molds; she had made it from a Jasper plaque of a Native American Indian.

From this mold, she made one of her most incredible pieces of jewelry—a huge sterling silver pendant with a piece of turquoise set into the necklace on the chief. I think my sister inherited the necklace—but my mom gave me the plaster mold.

This ring that I found in one of my inherited boxes from the shop sure looked like a lost wax piece. I even thought it could have been a ring that my grandmother made because she made a lot of silver rings. I finally decided that she had not made it because she typically cast in sterling silver or gold and this ring was just pot metal—costume, not fine, jewelry.

It was a really neat ring that was very mid-century modern and I knew that this angle would really help to sell it. The ring was also adjustable. It was only marked $8.50 in our antiques store, but it ended up selling for $35.67! What a cool piece, and it helped me to learn about lost wax casting. I am glad it didn't get lost in all my inherited boxes of stuff!

# #20 De Simone Pitcher

$3.00 **Paid**
**From:** Thrift store

**Desimone Italy Pitcher JUG Mod Eames Bird Picasso Rare!**

### Description:
Desimone Pitcher is unique and rare. Great piece because it is signed on the side instead of the base. The signature goes down the side by the handle. 6" height by 7.5" width with the handle by 5". Very mid century modern and Picasso in style. Very unique with the signature on the side. It is off white with brown, orangish red, yellow, green and blue. In excellent condition. No chips no cracks no crazing. Some small areas around the upper lip with uneven glaze. 1960s to 1970s I would guess.

**Winning Bid:** $305.00

**Ended:** 9/14/05
**History:** 28 bids
**Starting Bid:** $9.99
**Winner:** Wellesley, MA

**Viewed**
000289 X

# De Simone Pitcher  #20

## The Story

As I sat down to write this story, my friend Lori had just arrived with her son Hunter to pick up her daughter Paige. Strange and quite a coincidence and I will tell you why. As you know, Paige is Indy's best friend; she was over for a play date. Lori's husband and Paige's father is also an antiques dealer. His name is Lou Scalise and I run into Lou all over town!

Not only do I see him every Saturday at garage sales, but I run into him in my thrift stores and sometimes even at Costco. Lou cruises around town with a cigarette holder in his mouth. No cigarette attached to the holder, just the hand-carved holder.

As you can guess, Lou is quite a character and another quirk is that he only drives red cars. He has about eight of them. A red Mercedes, a red Yukon, a red BMW, a red RV and the list goes on. When I bought a red car at a garage sale to sell on eBay and it didn't get any bids, the first person I wanted to call was Lou. Lori said to me, "Don't you dare!"

So, let's get back to my story and how this all ties in together. I go to Pilates every Monday and Wednesday at 9 am. On my way home at 10 am, I stop by one of my favorite thrift stores.

So I walk in and hear this raspy voice ask, "What are you doing here? Find anything good lately?" I look up to see Lou with his cigarette holder and just have to smile. I say, "You know, Lou, I have never found anything great here." He agreed, and I picked up a pitcher from the front counter.

It was only $3 and looked like a Picasso painting. I decided to buy it. Wouldn't you just know that after uttering those discouraging words I would find a major score? But is that bad? I don't think so.

I got the pitcher home and saw that it was signed "Desimone" down the side. I did some research and found that it might be valuable. Awesome!

Giovanni De Simone (I probably should have made Desimone into two words—but it didn't seem to hurt me) was the founder of Ceramiche De Simone pottery. He was a painter, sculptor, writer and beloved husband. He was also the father of Rosita, Susanna, and Margherita, who currently run the company.

He was also Picasso's friend! Did I nail that one in my description or what? According to Giovanni's daughters, their father always told them the story of the ancient Greeks who came to the isle of Sicily to colonize it. With them, they brought an expert potter, and Giovanni was believed to be his descendent.

Giovanni created many new designs and patterns inspired by those ancient times. The De Simone family's pottery, with its hand-painted colors, is well-known and loved around the world for its boldness and modernity. Just like Picasso's art!

You can see all of this in the wonderful jug that I sold on eBay for over $300! By the way, Lou's family comes from the same region in Italy that this jug is from. Too cool!

# #21   Rose Bowl Ashtray

$0.²⁵
**Paid**
**From:** Thrift store

**Vintage Rose Bowl Ashtray UCLA 1950's Eames Pasadena**

**Description:**
Vintage ashtray says "Rose Bowl," does not say Pasadena or UCLA. 5¾" by 5¼" by 1¼". There is one nick and it needs cleaning. Neat vintage Eames era 1950s or so piece.

**Winning Bid:**

$16.⁰⁶
**Ended:** 9/14/05
**History:** 4 bids
**Starting Bid:** $9.99
**Winner:** Martinez, CA

**Viewed**
000033 X

# Rose Bowl Ashtray   #21

## The Story

This story cracks me up. I thought by positioning this 25-cent thrift store find as a UCLA memorabilia item it would sell better. It didn't even say UCLA on it! What was I thinking? And as many of you know, I am a USC alumna, so it was really very hard for me to market it in that manner. I should have followed my gut, because the guy who bought it is a Cal Bear alumnus. You just never know!

FYI, I have been buying and selling a ton of vintage ashtrays lately. I used to overlook them, but have learned that even if they don't sell at auction, they will eventually sell from my store at $9.99.

It is kind of crazy, but when I moved home to run my grandmother's antiques store in 1993, the first thing I did was to classify her entire store by category (just as eBay asks us to do). I learned to organize merchandise in this way as a buyer at May department stores. So, after painting the whole place white, I started a specific shelf for teacups, one for brass, one for cloisonné, one for depression glass, one for ashtrays, and the list goes on and on and on.

What is interesting is where I positioned the ashtrays in terms of actual real estate. The ash tray shelf (and I have often debated this—is "ashtray" one word or two?) was really hard to find. I actually forgot about it when the shop was open. The shelf was at ground level in a very narrow aisle. I don't think anyone who was actually looking for ashtrays would have found them, and I doubt they were ever noticed by a casual browser. We didn't sell a lot of ashtrays.

But with eBay, no matter where you position the physical product, someone can always find it easily with a keyword search. Amazing, isn't it? This is one of the big reasons that eBay works even better than having a retail store. Finding the ashtray was just what our buyer did and his story was great. Here is his email:

> When I was a little kid, my parents took us to Southern California to visit relatives. As we drove past the Rose Bowl, my dad pointed to it and said, 'Take a good look. You won't see that again for a long time.' I had no idea how long it would be.
>
> I started as an undergrad at Cal in 1962, while the memory of the 1959 Rose Bowl was still fresh. And I am still waiting for our next one. Two close calls and one outright robbery, but we still haven't been there. I bought the ashtray as just a Rose Bowl memento—nothing to do with UCLA.

I liked this guy, and WOW—over 45 years without a Rose Bowl appearance! That must just kill the Cal Bear alumni. I wish them luck for a Rose Bowl appearance—but only when USC is in the national championship somewhere else. And by the way, my 25-cent investment turned into $16.06. Over 64 times my original investment. That is better than a lot of my $1 purchases!

Ashtrays

# #22  Kodak Tripod

$10.00
**Paid**
**From:** Charity sale
Bellingham, WA

## Folmer Kodak 1903 Crown Camera Tripod No 2 NEAT

### Description:

Folmer Schwing Kodak Camera tripod is very neat and folds down to only 33" long. When it is extended it is about 4' 8" tall. You can adjust the height with the screw knobs. The markings say "Folmer & Schwing Div. Eastman Kodak Co. Rochester NY Crown Tripod No 2 Patented June 23, 1903." I think this one is very close to that date. I would guess 1903 to 1920s. Very nice. Someone has mounted a new fitting on the top, probably to use it with modern cameras. We still have the antique top piece and you can see it in one of the photos. In very good condition for its age. There may be a few minor splits in the wood.

**Winning Bid:** $42.78

**Ended:** 9/14/05
**History:** 4 bids
**Starting Bid:** $9.99
**Winner:** Hillsborough, NJ

**Viewed**
000136 X

# Kodak Tripod #22

## The Story

I was in Bellingham for a couple weeks of the summer and for that (surprisingly successful) book signing. I try to be in Bellingham every August for my mom's birthday and there is always one amazing charity sale around that time. It is held at the ice skating rink and I ALWAYS find awesome stuff. If you read the first *100 Best* book, you will remember the vase #93 that I paid $5 for and sold for $610. Pretty cool!

So, my mom and I were there early, waiting in line. We struck up a conversation with this really interesting lady ahead of us. Her name was Michelle Nolan and she was a book expert. I know literally nothing about books and she was fascinating. We came to find that she was also a lifestyle writer for *The Bellingham Herald*.

My mom is one of my greatest supporters, and she started pitching me as a lifestyle article to Michelle. I felt sorry for her, because once my mom gets going there is no stopping her. Quite a good trait! Michelle seemed receptive and I told her I would drop off a couple of my books at the *Herald* on Monday. One of Michelle's hesitations about even considering me for an article was that the lifestyle articles must be written about Whatcom County residents.

Well, let's see, I grew up in Bellingham, my grandmother lived there for 55 years, my dad and sister still live there and I spend between three weeks and three months there every summer. In fact, I still own a home there. Michelle thought that was great! And it was time for the sale to start.

In we rushed and grabbed our shopping carts. One of the pieces I found was this Kodak tripod. It was $10 and I thought it looked really interesting. I put it in my shopping cart along with a ton of other stuff.

On Monday the first thing I did was to drop off the books with Michelle. Walking into the *Herald* building brought back a lot of memories. My grandmother used to place a lot of ads with that newspaper. She was also written up a lot over the years.

The next thing I knew, Michelle's editor called to say they wanted to write an article. How exciting!

I met with Michelle at a Denny's for the interview. The *Herald* also wanted to have one of their photographers take some pictures at my grandmother's antiques store. Well, guess what? It was long gone. I still owned a house on Nevada Street, though, and it was empty, so I said, "Why don't we do the shoot there?"

While I was waiting for the photographer, I took the photos of the tripod for my eBay listing. The photographer showed up and he turned out to be Phil Dyer, a man who had taken many pictures of my grandmother and myself over the years for the *Herald*. We wrapped up our photo shoot and I packed the tripod to go back to California with me so Mo could ship it out when I returned.

I paid a lot for the tripod — $10 — but sold it for over $40, plus I got a feature article in the *Herald*. Can't get better than that. Or can it?

# #23 Gold Watch

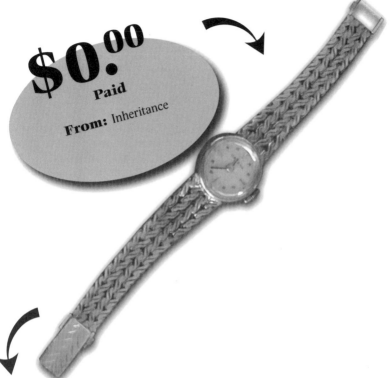

**$0.⁰⁰ Paid**

**From:** Inheritance

## Geneva Corletto 18k Gold Ladies Wristwatch Band Lovely

### Description:

This watch and the band are 18k. The watch is marked "Geneva 18kt Italy" and the band is marked "18k Corletto 0750 Italy." The band is 7¼" by ⅜". The watch itself is ¾ by ⅝". It is quite heavy and there is a lot of value in the gold. It weighs about .9 oz and my brother did the calculations like this..... .9 oz is about .8 oz troy which is the gold measure. Gold is $440 an ounce and 18 k is 75% pure, so melt amount is close to .8*.75*$440 or about $264. We figure $264 in gold melt. My brother, who is GIA (Gemological Institute of America certified) has checked and helped identify this piece.

**Winning Bid:**

# $330.⁰⁰

**Ended:** 9/15/05
**History:** 2 bids
**Starting Bid:** $299
**Winner:** Rochester, NY

**Viewed**
**000072 X**

# Gold Watch #23

## The Story

My grandmother loved cash, gold and her grandkids (not necessarily in that order). Any excess cash she had she did one of three things with. She hid it (I think she didn't put it in the bank because she had lived through the Depression), bought inventory for the shop, or bought gold. She loved to invest in gold because it was a commodity that didn't have to be tied to a piece of paper.

It wasn't a certificate of stock that she had to place in a safe deposit box. It was an actual piece of jewelry or a gold coin that she could play with. She liked to play the gold market, because to her it was a sure thing and would eventually go up in value. In the meantime, she had beautiful pieces of jewelry.

I think she got a huge kick out of hiding money in white envelopes all over the house. She hid cash under the tablecloth on the dining room table she used as a desk, in pockets of her clothing, and in shoe boxes. She was as sharp as a tack and knew where it all was and what it added up to. Once in a while we would find an envelope that she didn't remember. She loved those kinds of surprises!

One day when I was living back in Bellingham, she said to us, "I want someone to clean out my closets. Donate the clothes that I don't need and see if there is anything valuable to save." My brother didn't want to do it and my sister didn't either, so I said, "Sure, why not?"

The first order of business was to check all her pockets, plus her secret pockets. What is a secret pocket? Every time my grandmother got a new poncho, jacket, or leisure suit (I did not agree with her choice of clothing, but as we all know clothes do not make the man—or woman), she asked my mother (the amazing seamstress) to add a secret pocket. These were to be used for travel and for hiding things. It was a brilliant idea.

So, I started patting down every polyester item in her closet. Yikes! I found about $500 hidden in her clothing in various pockets. She gave me a bonus that day of $100.

My grandmother was always very generous with us and believed in sharing the wealth. The reason she worked hard was to be able to do nice things for others. That $100 was a very nice thing and all the wonderful things she left us in our inheritance were another very nice thing. I got this watch from her. It was just a piece that she had bought to invest in for the gold value. I put it on eBay with a description of how much gold was in it, and luckily it sold for more than the melt price!

After my grandmother passed away, Teresa Meurs, who was running the estate sales for us, came downstairs to give us an envelope filled with $200 in cash that one of the shoppers had found tucked in the bottom of a shoe box. What an honest man, and what a grandma I had. To see that white envelope with her handwriting that said 10-10's=$100, 5-20's=$100 with the total $200 made me very sad.

# #24 Solar Tea Jar

$0.50 Paid

**From:** Thrift store

## 1960's Op Art Orange Solar Iced Tea Bubble Jar COOL!

**Description:**
Neat iced ice tea bubble jar could be considered Eames era. 7" by 9" and in good to very good condition. Needs cleaning.

Winning Bid:

$9.99

**Ended:** 9/30/05
**History:** 1 bid (sold in store)
**Starting Bid:** $9.99
**Winner:** Noble, OK

Viewed

000052 X

# Solar Tea Jar #24

## The Story

I thought this solar tea jar was very mod and op art so I bought it for 50 cents at a thrift store. Just what is "op art?" "Op art" is a term used to describe items from the 1960s. "Op art" is short for "optical art," which was all the rage in 1965. Remember the peace and love decade? I don't, because I wasn't born yet, but maybe you do (just kidding).

Highlights of this era were the 1964 New York World's Fair, miniskirts, Star Trek, and Woodstock. Another highlight was the first man walking on the moon in 1969. Collectibles from this era are favorites on eBay.

I originally listed the tea jar in June, and it was for sale at auction while we were exhibiting at eBay Live. When Mo and I were getting packed to go to eBay Live, we needed some type of jar to put on the counter to collect business cards. Mo grabbed this one. It would now be semi-famous.

Well, it didn't sell at auction, so we listed it in my eBay store. We knew that with all the eBay love it had received at eBay Live (not to mention the exposure) that it would eventually sell.

After 30 days in my eBay store, it sold for $9.99 to Kent in Oklahoma. Kent wrote to me:

I owned one of these back in the early 1970s and used it a lot. Whatever happened to it is beyond me. It's kind of like a song you really liked when you were in high school; after years pass, you get older, but every time you hear that song, you are back in high school all over again.

Now with eBay, I think of things from my past and actually have access to them again! I now own six of these—four that I use as canisters and the other two... I use to make sun tea! Lots of my friends see them and say, 'I remember when I had one of those...' Yours was the start of my collection. For that, I thank you!

I have been telling you all along that people are trying to buy their childhoods. Now do you believe me? In fact, it appears that they are also trying to relive their high school years—I hadn't known that!

Goosebumps! And all from a $9.99 sale. No big money maker here, but what a heartwarming story. Remember that making a living on eBay isn't necessarily about the big hits. I sell about 600 ten- to twenty-dollar items each month and I make a great living. It is the singles and the doubles that pay the bills. Once in a while, you get a home run, but don't ever turn your nose up at a $10 item. You may have just made someone's day! ☺

# #25  Chevy Street Slam

$75.00 Paid

From: eBay Resellers Pallet

## Chevy Street Slam Silverado Ride on Power Wheels NEW

### Description:

Chevy Street Slam comes new in box. A dialed-up version of the Chevy Silverado. The changes include a rich magenta color, vacuum metalized grill and hub caps, and a hood scoop. This is a 12 volt, 2 seat vehicle with grass performance. An awesome toy! Ages 3 to 7. We bought some toy overstocks lately and this one of them. This item can not be returned to us and all questions must be directed to the manufacturer Power Wheels...Fisher Price. New in the box but there are some dings/cuts and dents/squishes in the box. Must be picked up in Palm Desert or you need to arrange for shipping. It is oversized, 60" by 34" by 22".

Winning Bid:

# $112.50

**Ended:** 10/10/05
**History:** 2 bids
**Starting Bid:** $99.99
**Winner:** USA

Viewed
000443 X

## The Story

This is a bittersweet story—kind of sad, yet still basically uplifting.

This car was one of the items that came on the pallet of toys I bought on eBay from the Reseller Marketplace that I talked about in story #16. The pallet had several ride-on vehicles, PlayStations and ESPN sports games. The folks at the Resellers Marketplace were showing that the retail for these items totaled $2,750, and the pallet was only bid up to $322.

I did my research and decided that I could most likely get about half of retail, or $1,375, on eBay. I then realized that I wouldn't need to make my usual five-to ten-times investment on these items because they were high-ticket and easy to sell. I decided I would be happy to double my money. I could therefore afford to spend about $687.50, plus a reasonable amount for shipping.

So I went in and placed my max bid of $687.50 and was thrilled to learn on June 27th that I had won the auction for $674.07!

This car came on a pallet with the other toys and sat for months (I'm not kidding) in my garage where my car should have been sitting. After I sold it the first time, it sat in my living room waiting for the buyer to arrange for shipping. He never did, even though the auction description had stated very clearly that the car was oversized and would not ship UPS or FedEX.

So after that auction, this huge box sat by my front door in my foyer (or "the lobby" as my mother now calls it) for another four months! Life as an eBay PowerSeller is never boring.

When it finally sold the second time, I was thrilled. I just wanted it gone. It was the summer that Mo was out of town, so the fact that the buyer didn't pay for it fell by the wayside. Finally, I went through our "waiting for money" book and noticed that payment for the car was long overdue—about 30 days.

I emailed the buyer and received no response. I waited another week and emailed again. This time, he sent immediate payment and arranged for shipping. He told me that the reason it had taken him so long to pay was because he had been in jail. I am guessing there is no Internet access in jail?

Now, I have heard every excuse in the book, but this one takes the cake. Whatever the buyer's crime was, it must have been pretty minor, because he had only been sent away for 30 days. He was buying the car for his son, and I think it must have made a very special gift. The father was released and so was I—free to move about my house!

# #26 Gumps Majolica Platter

$8.00 Paid
From: eBay Resellers Pallet

**Gumps Grape Leaf Majolica Platter Italy MIB LOVELY Pink**

### Description:
Gumps grape leaf platter is mint in the original box and is lovely. 17 by 13" and very highly detailed. I love the edge work and the hand painting. It is marked "Made in Italy." Gift item. Also marked with "Ceramiche Artisistiche B'Artigiana Bassano Del Grappa." Pinks and greens. Comes in the original box and in excellent condition. This item will ship in the box from the company and will show the contents on the outside. I have lots and lots of new in box gift items up for sale from world famous Gumps (San Francisco). These are all very high quality items and all have never been used.

**Winning Bid:**

# $73.85

**Ended:** 10/11/05
**History:** 10 bids
**Starting Bid:** $24.99
**Winner:** Summerville, SC

**Viewed**
 000082 X

# Gumps Majolica Platter #26

## The Story

I get a lot of "how to sell on eBay"-related questions submitted through the "Ask seller a question" links on my eBay auctions. These questions are really supposed to be about specific items, but a lot of eBayers see those links as an opportunity to ask me general questions about eBay selling, and quite frankly I don't blame them.

As I write more and more books and put out a weekly ezine, however, it has become increasingly difficult to answer all the questions. I am a people pleaser, and not answering each and every question is hard for me. Yikes! But to personally answer all the questions I get would be a full-time job.

One question I hear a lot is, "Do you think people buy more from you because you have written eBay books?" I always answer, "No, I don't think it helps, but I also don't think it hurts."

When I was putting this book together, I emailed buyers of all the featured items to see if they had any interesting back stories to share. The story behind this majolica platter (part of the pallets of Gumps merchandise I had bought) was quite interesting. I really liked this platter because the pallet included twelve of them, and they all sold for really great money.

Majolica is heavy earthenware that has been molded (as opposed to hand-formed). It is then decorated in rich colors with either a lead or tin glaze, which is usually very glossy and shiny. Majolica was very popular in the Victorian era, but continues to be extremely collectible today. Most of the

majolica that I find comes from Italy, Spain and Portugal.

The lady who purchased this piece shared her story with me:

> I really love the platter. When I first discovered it, I had just finished reading your first *100 Best* book and decided to check out your auctions. I'm a majolica collector, so when I saw that gorgeous platter in my favorite colors, I bid on it and won it. When it arrived, its beauty went beyond my expectations, and I was particularly pleased with the quality.
>
> The great part is that I am attempting to teach my five-year-old granddaughter Emma to appreciate beautiful majolica platters as well as old buttons, tea sets and dolls, just like your grandmother taught you. This platter is just a little piece of the universe that inspires me. I'm moved by the great spirit of eBay sellers like you who are willing to share the joy and success that eBay brings them and by grandmothers who take the time to pass that joy on to the little ones. I want to be that grandmother! Thanks for letting me share. -Cynthia

Goosebumps! I can tell Cynthia is already the wonderful grandmother she aspires to be. (By the way, she doesn't look old enough to be a grandmother). Not only that, but I was wrong—writing eBay books definitely drives customers to my auctions. How cool is that?

# #27  Coralene Nippon Vase

$4.00
Paid
From: Garage sale

**Nippon Coralene Moriage Antique Burmese Vase Floral WOW**

**Description:**
Lovely Nippon vase is amazing; signed with the #242 signature from Van Patten's book, "U.S. Patent BR 912171 Feb. 9 1909" and then some Japanese characters. These tightly-spaced glass beads have a 3-dimensional look. This vase is 5¼" by 4¾" tall, 1¼" at the mouth. Double handles. A beautiful green and pink coloration which doesn't show up as well in the photos as it does in person. The coloration reminds me of Burmese. I would date this to the 1910s to 1920s. There is slight wear to the piece: 4 chips at the ruffled edge and a very fine hairline in one of the handles. Some slight wear to the coralene pattern close to the base. There is wear to the gold on the handles and at the neck and base. The workmanship is exquisite.

**Winning Bid:** $39.00

**Ended:** 10/13/05
**History:** 8 bids
**Starting Bid:** $9.99
**Winner:** Northridge, CA

Viewed
000390 X

# Coralene Nippon Vase  #27

## The Story

My mom and I were at a community sale at some condos in Rancho Mirage. It was a great neighborhood, but condo sales do not tend to be the best. We had made the rounds and were about to leave when we saw an arrow going way into the center of the complex. We said, "What the heck," and off we went.

When we walked in to the sale, we saw stickers on many items that said "Make Offer," and this vase was one of those items. There isn't much I dislike more than "Make Offer" stickers, unless it's sellers who start talking about what things are worth on eBay. But when the sellers did start talking, what they told us was even worse: their aunt had died, and they had hired a professional estate seller to come in and take the best items from her estate. This sale included only the leftovers, or "dregs" (one of my grandmother's oft-used words). Oh boy!

Anyway, even professional estate sellers and professional eBay dealers (like me) don't (and can't) know everything. I am the first to admit that. My grandmother always said she wasn't an expert and that there were really no such things as experts.

I really liked this vase and made a pile that included it and some really interesting jewelry—stuff my grandma would have loved. I said, "How much?" The sellers wouldn't name a price, so I waited it out—you know me! Finally, they said, "How about $10 for the bunch?" Score! You just never know. So I bought it all.

Even though this vase was in "as is" condition, I had a great feeling about it. It looked like some type of art glass to me. It wasn't signed "Nippon," but as soon as I got it home, I typed in the patent number on Google and all the information I needed was right there at my fingertips.

This patent was granted on Feb. 9 1909 to Alban L. Rock, a U.S. citizen who lived in Yokohama, Japan, for the coralene glass bead effect. I had often heard my grandmother talk about coralene.

Coralene was made by painting a picture or design onto the glass with syrupy enamel paint. Then tiny glass balls were applied to this surface and re-heated so they partially melted into the surface. The result looked a little like the rough surface of coral and was often used in a coral design.

Another great lesson I learned from my grandmother was, "Whenever you acquire an interesting piece, always buy a book." I immediately jumped on Amazon and bought Van Patten's *The ABC's of Collecting Nippon*. It helped me with my description. Even though the vase was chipped, I still thought it would bring $100.

I started the bidding at $9.99 and was a little disappointed when it only sold for $39. I had invested a lot of my time and effort in this item, and I thought it was a winner. As is the way of eBay, a different item that I purchased at that same sale turned out to be the star (hint: see #28).

On the other hand, I had only spent $4, and now I owned a new book for my growing library—thanks to my grandmother's always-awesome advice!

# #28  Alexander Ritchie Brooch

$1.⁰⁰ **Paid**

**From:** Garage sale

## Silver Brooch AR Iona Alexander Ritchie Celtic Rare!

### Description:
Silver brooch is unique. A round brooch in the shape of a silver sword and shield. 1⅝" round. Signed with stamped "A.R." and "IONA." This stamp is the mark of Alexander Ritchie. He is a famous designer who made wonderful jewelry and silver pieces in the early part of the 1900s on the tiny isle (island) of Iona. Highly collectible. It is very art deco and arts and crafts. Not marked sterling, but I believe it is. Scottish Celtic Revival type brooch. I am guessing about 1910. This is a wonderful piece in great condition.

**Winning Bid:** $330.⁰⁰

**Ended:** 10/21/05
**History:** 7 bids
**Starting Bid:** $9.99
**Winner:** UK

**Viewed**
000504 X

# Alexander Ritchie Brooch  #28

## The Story

This piece came with the handful of jewelry and the Nippon vase that I purchased all for $10! I had put this piece into the pile because it looked intriguing. The workmanship was special, but I didn't think the brooch was sterling because it didn't have any of the standard "sterling" markings: the word "sterling," the numbers 800 to 925 (indicating percentage of pure silver content), or a rampant lion hallmark.

Typically, the better jewelry pieces will be done in sterling, gold or platinum. I didn't have high hopes for this brooch, but decided to do some research on it anyway.

I typed "AR Iona" into my computer and did a completed auction search on eBay. I couldn't believe it, but this was a good piece of jewelry! The AR pieces sold for hundreds-of-dollars.

"AR" stands for Alexander Ritchie, and "Iona" for the tiny island of Iona, off the west coast of Scotland. Iona is famous for its Celtic crosses and carvings. People who visit Iona say it has an extraordinary spiritual atmosphere that feels almost magical.

Alexander and his wife Euphemia lived a remarkable life. They began making crafts in 1898, but didn't live permanently on Iona until 1909. The ancient carvings they found on the island inspired them in their attempts to create magnificent Celtic crafts. They worked not only in sterling, but also in wood, brass and copper. They specialized in silver brooches and only made items of the highest quality.

A brooch (which rhymes with "poach," not "pooch") is a decorative pin. The name comes from the French word "broche" which means "to pierce," a reference to the pin that is used to secure the brooch in place.

Alexander Ritchie married Euphemia Thompson in 1898, when he was 42. In one of his letters, he writes that they had married "on very little except hope...but...my wife being an expert with the pencil, we began to adapt Iona designs to silver, and have had as much success as I can expect." Little did he know that he would become one of the most reknowned Scottish silversmiths of his time.

Euphemia passed away in 1941. Two days later, Alec followed her. They were buried together in the burial ground of the Kings on Iona. Theirs was a great love story, just like my grandma and grandpa's.

As far as I could figure, this piece was made between 1900 and 1920. According to the Ritchie website, "Many 1920s and earlier Ritchie silver items have no hallmark whatsoever, just the letters 'AR' and 'Iona,' usually impressed in two separate rectangles." That was my piece! It turned out that it was most likely sterling.

What a score! Out of the dregs of an estate sale that had been professionally picked over, I found a true treasure and a little piece of heaven! It sold for $330, and was shipped back across the ocean to the United Kingdom. At least it is getting closer to its magical birthplace on the Isle of Iona.

# #29 Sterling Stamp Locket

## Sterling Silver Stamp Locket Antique English AE Jones

**Description:**

This locket is hallmarked with a rampant lion for sterling silver and what looks like a thistle in a shield and an "E" or a musical sign. Also has the initials "AEJ." We would like to know the maker if anyone knows. A nice eBayer writes, "It was Albert Edward Jones, a renowned Birmingham silversmith from about 1900 onward. This piece is hallmarked for Chester (in the NW of England) for 1905." Such a cute locket in the shape of an envelope. Says "Stamps" in script on the front. A little bent and needs polishing. A darling little piece. 1" by 1" by ⅛". I would guess 1890s to 1920s.

**Winning Bid:**

# $29.⁸⁸

**Ended:** 10/21/05
**History:** 4 bids
**Starting Bid:** $9.99
**Winner:** New Zealand

**Viewed**
`000072` X

# Sterling Stamp Locket  #29

## The Story

This was another of the little gems that I bought in the $10 pile! You just never know. This piece was just darling and something my grandmother would have loved. You see, any time an envelope arrived in the mail, she cut off the stamp or stamps and kept them in a baggy in her desk. Believe me, nothing ever went to waste with that lady.

I always thought it was strange that my grandmother recycled everything and even kept old used postage stamps. Whatever!

Then, when I turned twelve, I became interested in stamp collecting. It all started when I found a United States stamp book filled with stamps in the old hallway of the shop. My grandmother was quick to start giving me bags and bags of those stamps she had saved over the years. I learned how to gently steam the stamps off of the paper, how to flatten them and then carefully attach them to the correct pages in the stamp collecting book. What a geek!

It turns out I wasn't the only geek in town. My friend Susan Thornberg (who lived across the street) and is now the editor of my *100 Best* books, was also a stamp collector.

I can't believe how many days after school we would get on the bus and ride to the Bellingham Stamp and Coin shop and spend hours poring over the stamps. My favorites were the foreign ones, because they were so colorful and exciting. I dreamed of far-off exotic locales and I especially loved fish stamps. I had a huge yellow and blue Ambassador stamp album that was bulging with cool stamps.

When I got to high school, I decided that stamp collecting was stupid and I sold that album for $20 at a garage sale. How sad is that? I wish I had it back. My grandmother always said, "I have never regretted anything that I have bought, only what I have sold."

This stamp locket was something that my grandmother would have kept. I just know it. I also know that I, personally, will sell anything (as long as it has no sentimental value) if I can make money. So I decided to sell the locket.

I couldn't figure out what "AEJ" stood for, so I put the locket on eBay with a question in the title and asked for help in the description. Not more than four hours passed before a nice eBayer sent this information: "Your stamp locket was made by Albert Edward Jones, a renowned Birmingham silversmith from about 1900 onward."

Albert Jones was born in 1878 into a family of English craftsman and by the age of fourteen had already decided to become a silversmith. In 1902, at the age of 24, he started his own business. Jones was inspired by the Arts and Crafts movement, which shows in the clean lines of his work, and success came quickly.

"A piece of silverwork to be really interesting must be endued with a spirit of art," Jones said in 1906 at the tender age of 28. He passed away in 1954 at the age of 76, but his legacy lives on in the beauty and timelessness of pieces like this darling locket that sold for almost $30.

# #30  Retro Pair Lamps

$2.00 Paid From: Garage sale

## Mid Century Danish Modern Eames 2 Table Lamps Lucite

### Description:

Mid-century lamps are very art deco and retro. This pair of table lamps is so neat. 9⅜" by 3⅞" and 7" to the top of the wood at the base of the socket. Lucite and blond wood and the curved wood is very hard to find. The Lucite pieces are stacked in the skyscraper design. Very Eames-era, geometric, vintage and space age. I can't wait to see them all fixed up with the right 1950s shades. They will be awesome! These need some tlc. There is wear and scratches. The metal is tarnished and it all needs cleaning. A couple of splits in the wood. They need rewiring.

**Winning Bid:**

$32.00

**Ended:** 10/21/05
**History:** 7 bids
**Starting Bid:** $3.99
**Winner:** Santa Monica, CA

**Viewed**

000222 X

# Retro Pair Lamps   #30

## The Story

I bought this pair of lamps at a garage sale for $2. So neat and unique. They were made of wood with Lucite plastic in the center. I fell in love with them even though they needed work. They were dirty, with some splits in the wood, and they definitely needed rewiring.

I could tell that they were very Eames era mid-century modern from the 1950s. A very collectible pair of lamps—people love lamps and they love mid-century modern. I didn't think I could miss.

The Lucite rings in the center of the lamp were stacked in the skyscraper style. Lucite is a clear strong plastic that could be molded or carved. It was very popular in the 1940s and 1950s for purses, jewelry and decoration on home furnishings.

Also, the Learning Annex in Los Angeles and San Diego had asked me to teach a one and a half hour course about selling antiques and collectibles on eBay for their "eBay Expo." (Much like the "Real Estate Expo" they do with Donald Trump in LA and NY.) Well, I hoped that it would be like his—he draws 25,000 people.

So, I was picking three items to talk about that would be listed on eBay while I was teaching the course. This was one of the three items that I chose. I started the auction at $9.99 and showed it in my PowerPoint presentation. Guess what? No one bid.

I was wrong about the Learning Annex "eBay Expo" also, because only about 50 people showed up—not quite 25,000. And I didn't even sell one of my three hot items that I used as a teaching tool!

It is funny, but people always say to me, "Well, you have an advantage, you grew up doing this for a living with your grandmother. How can I ever learn what you know or get to your level?"

Once again, just so you all know this, even though I have been doing this my entire life (well, almost), I still can't predict correctly what is going to sell or for how much. That is why it is so much fun! And that is exactly the reason that you all can be just as successful!

So, after I taught the course and was back home in Palm Desert, I relisted the pair of lamps starting at $3.99. I was very pleased to find that they actually sold this time! And for $32. It always surprises me because someone could have had them the week before for only $9.99.

So once again, eBay amazes me and I hope to someday be amazed by teaching 25,000 of you about eBay in my own eBay expo—Just like Donald Trump!

# #31 Jean Manley Figurines

**$10.⁰⁰/6**
Paid
From: Garage sale

## European Art Barker Bros Eames Small Girl Figurine HELP

### Description:

This is a small girl figurine; smaller matching figurine also up for sale in separate auction. HELP. Who made it? 6¼" by 3½" by 1½". This one has a "Barker Bros" tag on the base with another tag saying "7737 BS." Little girl is in a blue dress with dots. She has blonde hair; her head is tilted and it has been broken off at the neck and repaired. Big rose bow in her hair. There is crazing and some nicks. I am guessing that this is Scandinavian or European art pottery. I would really like more information. I got six of these figurines from a garage sale; two of them had old price stickers from Barker Bros. Barker Bros was a very upscale furniture store in Los Angeles that opened in 1924. I am guessing that these pieces are 1950s or so Eames era but I couldn't find out when Barker Bros closed its doors.

**Winning Bid:** **$159.³³/6**

**Ended:** 10/21/05
**History:** 32 bids/6
**Starting Bid:** $9.99/6
**Winners:** LA, Livermore, Venice, all CA

**Viewed**
`000390` X

# Jean Manley Figurines #31

## The Story

There was a garage sale in a pretty good part of Palm Desert. It appeared to be an estate sale, and the items, including some figurines, were really intriguing, but they were not cheap. The women running the sale were very firm with their prices, which is probably why there were still a lot of items left three hours into the sale.

One of the first things I noticed were six ceramic figurines of little girls and women. They were very crudely made, but there was something about them that stood out. They had a certain charm and appeal. I had a hunch that they were made by someone famous. None of them were signed, however.

On the base of several of them was an old price tag from Barker Brothers in LA. I thought they were definitely retro Eames era and figured that I couldn't lose for $2 each. I asked the ladies if they would consider $10 for all six pieces, since I was buying in bulk. After hemming and hawing for several minutes, they finally agreed. "They drove a hard bargain," as my grandmother would have said.

I got home and put the figurines on eBay with "Help" in the title. I identified them as Scandinavian or European. I couldn't have been more wrong. With less than twelve hours to go in the auctions, I got an email saying that they were probably made by California potter Jean Manley. Wow! I knew that these were good.

Maureen's husband was on his way over to get help in selling a convertible. I was going to take the pictures and help him list it. We had to call and stall him because I needed time to modify my auction listings. With less than twelve hours left in the auctions, eBay would not allow me to change the auction descriptions of items that already had bids. All I could do was add to the descriptions.

So I quickly went in and added to the descriptions in the auctions that had bids. I ended the auctions with no bids early so that I could immediately relist them with the name "Jean Manley" in the title. Whew! It was a stressful hour here at The Q of A.

The nice eBayer who had identified them for me suggested that I contact Jack Chipman in Venice, CA for authentication. I emailed him and he immediately wrote back to verify that yes, they were Jean Manley pieces. I sent him a copy of my first *100 Best* book as a thank you and Jack ended up buying two of the figurines that I relisted! Here is an email he sent:

> My interest in Jean Manley is two-fold. First I'm a California pottery collector and I enjoy the doll-like simplicity and muted glaze colors Manley used in her figures. My second reason for purchasing your examples is to add to the cache of photos for when I need to update one of my six reference books. I'm considered by many to be the 'godfather' of California pottery after writing the first book on the subject, *Collector's Encyclopedia of California Pottery*.

How cool is that? The Godfather of California Pottery shopping with The Queen of Auctions. It can't get any stranger than this! By the way, the Manley figurine that sold for the most (at $44.99) had a broken neck and didn't have "Manley" in the auction title. Go figure.

# #32 Art Glass Italian Lady

**$10.⁰⁰** Paid

From: Garage sale

## Italian Art Glass Murano Eames Lady Figurine Big Hat ?

**Description:**

Italian art glass lady figurine has a big hat on. This is an awesome statue or figurine. 15.5" by 4.75". Quite large. The woman has a yellow hat, white body, gold hair, a blue and green outfit and red shoes. Semi-nude and in excellent condition. Blown glass and I am guessing Murano. If anyone knows anything we would appreciate knowing. I would guess 1940s to 1980s which could possibly be Eames era. No chips no cracks no crazing. A few popped bubbles on the pant legs. Venini? Fratelli Toso? Viennale?

**Winning Bid: $1,125.⁰⁰**

**Ended:** 10/21/05
**History:** 12 bids
**Starting Bid:** $9.99
**Winner:** Venezia, Italy

**Viewed**
000211 X

# Art Glass Italian Lady #32

## The Story

After buying the six darling figurines that turned out to be Jean Manley pieces, I took a closer look at this huge glass figurine on the table. It was priced at $10, which I thought was high for a garage sale, but once again, there was just something about it. I couldn't put my finger on it and the age of this piece eluded me.

She could have been new or 1940s retro. With blown glass it is really hard to tell. There wasn't much wear on the base and there were no signatures. Since the six pottery figurines had the vintage Barker Bros. price tags (I could guess that those price tags were probably from the 1950s), I took a leap of faith and decided that this piece might just be vintage also.

The glass lady appeared very risque with her low cut top, but she wasn't a newer item. She seemed to be pushing the boundaries of what was allowed in a piece of art without going over the line. That fact and her big hat reminded me of the 1940s and yet I still couldn't put a definitive date on her. I knew that she was an incredible figurine made from blown glass and that the attention to detail and larger size would have made her an expensive piece originally. I just had to take a chance on her for the $10 asking price.

I positioned her as a piece of Italian art glass, which was my gut feeling. I gave a date range from 1940 to 1980 to protect myself and guessed that the piece was made on the island of Murano, which is just across from Venice.

The auction for this figure was ending right about the same time as the Manley figurines. We had gotten a lot of inquiries about it—from California to Europe—but the bidding was only up to about $100 when Maureen's husband Paul arrived to get some help in selling his convertible.

Paul and I went outside and took a bunch of photos and then came back in to list it. The work went quickly and I let Paul do most of it from Maureen's desk. While he was typing away, I took a peek at this figurine. It was up to $330 with just 35 minutes left. Wow!

Paul and Mo had left, and I continued to watch the auction. That is the problem when you get a runner like this—you can't leave the house. You want to sit and refresh and refresh the computer screen up until the bitter end. So that is what I did. I couldn't believe it when the lady ended up selling for $1,125 in the last few seconds!!! It was so fun to watch.

I immediately called Maureen and Paul to tell them. I do believe in karma and because I helped Paul with the car that day, I think I got a little bit of good karma thrown back at me in the form of this auction.

By the way, while she was listed on eBay, we had a small earthquake. I ran from my bedroom to make sure my kids were OK and then went immediately into my eBay room and she was the first thing I grabbed. Pathetic!

The strange part of the story is that the man who bought it was from Italy, and we ended up shipping her back to Venice. She now lives right across the canal from Murano, the very place I had guessed that she had been made.

# #33 TI MBA Calculator

$0.<sup>50</sup> Paid

From: Thrift store

**Texas Instruments Vintage The MBA Electronic Calculator**

## Description:

Texas Instruments Calculator TI is the MBA model. 6" by 3". Needs cleaning and I don't know if it works because I don't have the plug. Really cute though for a Masters in Business Administration degree holder. I would guess from the 1970s to 1980s. Marked "421159 ATA 09 USA" on the back side.

**Winning Bid:** $12.<sup>49</sup>

**Ended:** 10/24/05
**History:** 2 bids
**Starting Bid:** $9.99
**Winner:** France

**Viewed**
000035 X

# TI MBA Calculator #33

## The Story

I was in my favorite thrift store and decided to check out the appliance section. I rarely go into this department, but I had been hearing so much about electronics and old calculators selling for big bucks that I did a quick run-through. And I had just finished my Wiley book that featured a Sharp calculator from the 1970s that sold for $217.50. I had calculators on the brain.

Right on the top of the pile was a Texas instruments calculator—the MBA version. It looked like one of the old Texas Instrument calculators that my grandma and I used to use on her desk, and besides that, it was an MBA.

I have my MBA, Masters in Business Administration, from the University of Southern California. I graduated in the spring of 1991 and my entire family flew down for the ceremony. How cool was that? My grandma (in her wheelchair) even came for this amazing event. So my dad, mom, brother, sister and grandmother all drove over to my townhouse in the valley for a celebration.

We had decided to host a brunch, and my grandmother offered to supply a turkey. Not just any turkey, but a turkey flown from Bellingham, WA. What—they don't have turkeys in Southern California? Of course they do, and my family still laughs about this today.

My grandmother was the ultimate coupon and sale shopper. Every Sunday when the ads came out she would start lists and begin cutting coupons. She had a list for every store in town, and (before she was in a wheelchair) she would drive to every one to get the best buys. We always joked that she was probably spending more money in gas than she saved in her shopping. Oh, yeah—if the store was out of the item, she would wait in line for a rain check and then return later in the week. She was so funny—it must have had something to do with living through the Depression!

So, in the weeks leading up to my graduation, she hunted all over Bellingham to find the best buy on the biggest turkey she could find. She made sure it was frozen and then somehow she conned my dad into carrying a frozen turkey onto Alaska Airlines as his carry on. Does this sound a little like the Bellingham Hillbillies?

I still can't believe that they brought a turkey from Bellingham—it seemed sort of normal at the time. Anyway, my graduation and the brunch were fantastic. I have never tasted such a good turkey!

So, I bought the MBA calculator even though it didn't have a power cord because it was only 50 cents and I put it up on eBay. I couldn't believe it when the calculator sold for $12.49 and then the gal who bought it paid another $11 to have it shipped to France! I guess if a turkey can come from Bellingham to Southern California to be eaten, a calculator can go from Southern California to France to be collected!

# #34  USC vs. WSU Football Tickets

**$140.<sup>00</sup>**

Paid

From: Ticket broker

## 2 USC vs. WSU Washington 10/29 Tickets NR 1 Day

**Description:**
2 USC Trojans vs WSU Washington 10/29 Tickets NR 1 Day! This is a one-day auction so bid now! Don't let these get away. Sold out homecoming game. Section 3 is not bad! They are section 3 row 82 and seats 3 and 4.

**Winning Bid:**

**$133.<sup>50</sup>**

Ended: 10/25/05
History: 16 bids
Starting Bid: $9.99
Winner: Redondo Beach, CA

Viewed
000058 X

# USC vs WSU Football Tickets #34

## The Story

Every year I try to take my kids to one home football game in Los Angeles. USC with Pete Carroll at the helm has been on a football roll lately, and when you are winning, there is no better place to be on a Saturday afternoon in the fall than in the LA Coliseum.

I bought eight tickets to the homecoming game from a ticket broker on the internet. It was going to be a great game because my mom and grandmother had gone to WSU and they were our opponents that weekend. I paid $70 per ticket and I got eight because I wasn't sure who would be in town for the event.

We often go with my friends Jeff and Joanne Carolan. Joanne and I were roommates when we lived in Madrid for a semester when I was at USC. She is hysterical and we call her Jo Bird. Then there were my two kids, possibly my brother, my mom, and my sister Kristin (Kiki), who was maybe going to be in town. So, eight tickets seemed like a safe bet and I know (as you probably do also) that if you have tickets you aren't going to use, eBay is a fantastic place to sell them.

My sister did decide to fly down for Halloween and the game. My brother agreed to attend this game (as his one-per-year contract states). Just kidding; he is not a big football fan, but usually appeases me with one appearance per year. My mom, me and my two kids would also be going. So, I had two tickets extra.

I quickly listed them on eBay in a one-day auction and started the bidding at $9.99. I was thrilled when they sold for $133.50 and I got almost all of my money back. It only cost me $6.50 (plus the eBay fees) to be safe rather than sorry!

The game was a blast and we stayed at the Bonaventure in LA, my kids' favorite hotel in the entire world. Nothing can compare to this hotel for my children. We had dinner upstairs in the rotating lounge, and that was a high point of the weekend until my sister announced that she was pregnant with her first child! I was going to be an aunt and my kids were going to have a cousin!

But, back to reality and the hotel situation. I am a Starwood preferred guest so I usually get a free upgrade at the Bonaventure. Well, this time there were three adults and two kids staying in a standard room—just two queen beds. And there were no upgrades available—the hotel was sold out. It was going to be tight quarters. My mom and Kiki shared a bed and I shared a bed with Indiana.

The room was so tiny, they couldn't even bring in a rollaway for Houston because of fire regulations. There was a skinny wooden ledge above the beds that we made into a sort of bed for him to sleep on. Needless to say, Houston didn't feel very rested the next day. Actually, none of us did, but it was an adventure at the Bonaventure that we still laugh about today! "Remember when Houston slept on the ledge?"

# #35  Ferragamo Leather Pumps

**$10.00** Paid

From: Katrina fundraiser

**Ferragamo Italian New Leather Pumps Shoes Blue 9.5 MIB**

### Description:

Ferragamo Italian New Leather Pumps Shoes are blue and a 9½ new in box. Beautiful midnight blue calf with patent leather toe and heel. Salvatore Ferragamo Florence. Navy pumps heels. The heel is about 2⅜" medium heel. The style is DS U 81830. Size is 9.5 or 9½ B. Faina is the style. There is one tiny crease in the leather by the heel. Otherwise perfect—never worn and super expensive. We have more auctions with expensive designer shoes in this same size also up for sale this week.

**Winning Bid:** **$51.00**

Ended: 10/25/05
History: 15 bids
Starting Bid: $9.99
Winner: Victoria, Australia

Viewed
000068 X

# Ferragamo Leather Pumps #35

## The Story

Hurricane Katrina formed over the Bahamas on August 23, 2005. It became one of the deadliest and costliest of all Atlantic-based hurricanes, causing devastation to many parts of the southern United States.

New Orleans was especially hard hit, and many of its residents were out of their homes and jobs. 80% of the city flooded and 1,836 people lost their lives. Damages from the storm were estimated at $81.2 billion, making it the costliest natural disaster in US history. It was a tragedy.

Here in the desert, employees at Saks Fifth Avenue banded together to hold a charity sale, with all proceeds benefiting their counterparts in New Orleans. What an amazing outpouring of time, effort, and love. My mom and I spent several days at this sale and ended up spending a lot of money.

The SFA employees had donated many items themselves and received donations from their customers. There were a lot of quality items. The prices were a bit high—but we knew the money was going to a great cause.

There were boxes and boxes of brand new designer shoes—all priced at $10 each. I bought about six pairs and thought these Ferragamo pumps were just spectacular.

I have always been fascinated with Hollywood, especially old Hollywood and the movie business. Someday, I will write or produce a movie. It is a dream of mine. So, I was thrilled to learn more about Salvatore Ferragamo and find that he was known as "The Shoemaker to the Stars."

Salvatore was born in 1899 near Naples, Italy. After making his first pair of shoes at the age of nine for his sister, he decided that he had found his calling. Salvatore started his career in Hollywood, California in the 1920s, initially creating shoe designs for Hollywood productions.

Feragamo's most celebrated pieces include Dorothy's ruby slippers for the Wizard of Oz. How cool is that?

No one knows for sure how many pairs of the ruby slippers were made for Judy Garland, her stand-in, and the Wicked Witch, but many pairs were rescued from the incinerator by a man named Kent Warner who worked at MGM's costume department in the 1960s. Warner was an interesting character and (most notably) a very successful treasure hunter. Isn't that what eBay is all about?

We do know that one pair of ruby slippers now sits in the Smithsonian and others have been sold for record amounts over the years!

Ferragamo left Hollywood in 1927 to settle in Florence. By the 1950s, his company was producing 350 pairs of handmade shoes each day! He passed away in 1960 at the age of 62, but his name lives on in an international fashion company that is still in business today.

These wonderful pumps sold for $51 and were shipped to Australia. The buyer, Nicky Melbourne of Victoria, Australia, writes, "I am still wearing those shoes. Thanks once again!"

So, they didn't sell for the $666,000 that a pair of ruby slippers brought at auction in 2000, but they did make me some money, made an Australian gal happy, and helped out the New Orleans Saks Fifth Avenue employees. An all-around great transaction. Now, if I could just find some ruby slippers......

# #36 Chenille Bedspread

$20.00
**Paid**
**From:** Katrina fundraiser

### Vintage Chenille Bedspread Peacock Eames Colorful!

**Description:**

Vintage bedspread is awesome. White background with yellow, green, pink, red and black. I would guess 1950s Eames era. There is some damage along the top edge—a few holes and it has had a repair job that should be done more professionally. The rest of it looks great. I have tried to show the damage in one of the photos. 80" by 96" so I am guessing that it is a twin. It has rounded corners on the lower edge—so I measured it the best that I could.

**Winning Bid:**

# $66.59

**Ended:** 10/31/05
**History:** 11 bids
**Starting Bid:** $9.99
**Winner:** Montgomery, AL

**Viewed**
000246 X

# Chenille Bedspread #36

## The Story

I paid a lot ($20) for this bedspread for two reasons. The first was because the money was going to the Katrina fundraiser and the second was because chenille bedspreads sell really well.

"Chenille" is derived from the French word for "caterpillar." The word "chenille," when properly pronounced, would be "shen-knee." Oooh—we sound so cosmopolitan! Chenille is produced by weaving a fabric using fuzzy or puffy yarn with pile protruding from all sides. It is extremely soft and the loops and bumps from the yarn create depth and texture.

This bedspread was definitely vintage and I loved the colorful peacock that adorned the top. I knew that I could get at least my $20 investment back, and that buying the bedspread from the Katrina charity sale would benefit those people in New Orleans who had lost their homes and jobs.

The bedspread measured 80" by 96", so I guessed that it was a twin. Typically, the larger size chenille (practice saying "shen-knee") spreads (doubles, queens and kings) sell the best. This one had some damage along the top edge, so I made sure to note that in the description.

I was thrilled when it sold for $66.59 to a buyer in Alabama. The email I got from the gal who purchased it tore at my heart strings:

I bought this bedspread for my mother for Christmas of 2005. We live in Alabama, whose gulf coast was devastated by Hurricane Katrina. My mom grew up there and bought two cottages on Mobile Bay to fix up. This was her 'empty nest project' and passion for several years.

She had just completed the renovations and decorating the cottages with treasures she had collected over the years. She is an avid antique and junk hunter. Well, Katrina swept away both her cottages, including some vintage chenille bedspreads she had there. My three sisters and I decided to try and replace some of her treasures for Christmas—the bedspreads, Lu Ray dishes etc. This bedspread was one of those gifts. She cried when she opened it and thinks it is beautiful! -Jordan McBride

Well, I am crying now. What an amazing email. When you aren't part of a natural disaster, you don't really realize the incredible impact that it can have on so many people's lives. What a beautiful thing those daughters did for their mother that Christmas. From a Katrina charity sale in California back to Alabama to replace an item lost in Katrina. Talk about a story making a full circle.

# #37  JP Gaultier Perfume Bottle

**$5.00**
Paid
**From:** Katrina fundraiser

## Jean Paul Gaultier Summer Perfume Kitsch Hawaiiana FAB

**Description:**
Perfume bottle is very cool and measures 6" by 1.75" by 2.5". It is the summer fragrance tester from Saks Fifth Avenue. It is still pretty full. 100 ml 3.3 ounces. Really neat and tropical in the shape of a female torso. In very good condition. I think that these were from the 1990s but I am not sure.

**Winning Bid:**

**$27.00**

**Ended:** 10/31/05
**History:** 6 bids
**Starting Bid:** $9.99
**Winner:** Atlanta, GA

Viewed
`000042` X

# JP Gaultier Perfume Bottle  #37

## The Story

I bought this neat looking perfume bottle at the same Katrina charity sale. Once again, $5 was a little steep, but it was for hurricane relief and the more money I could spend that day, the better! This perfume bottle was a tester right off of the Saks Fifth Avenue counter.

I have heard incredible tales of certain perfume bottles selling in the $1,000 range. One brand that typically sells for a lot of money is Lalique. Lalique is a French crystal company and their perfume bottles are works of art. I'm still looking for my Lalique!

I knew that this Jean-Paul Gaultier bottle was no Lalique, but it was really kitschy and had a Hawaiian flair. Kitsch sells. Kitsch is defined as "art that is mass produced in order to pander to public demand." Typically the art is in poor taste ("kitsch" literally means "worthless" in German). Kitsch, however, has been made popular in recent years because of pop art. A lot of objects that might formerly have been dismissed as "kitschy" are now revered by collectors as "camp." Examples include Elvis painted on velvet, garden gnomes, and anything that might be described as "Hawaiiana."

Hawaii and tropical is very collectible. So this perfume bottle had quite a few things going for it. It was figural (in the shape of a woman's bust), it was kitschy, and it was tropical.

Jean-Paul Gaultier also has quite a following. He was born in 1952 in France and worked for Pierre Cardin at the start of his career. He set up his own label in 1976, rejecting his training in favor of a style that was based on the London street scene. He is known as the *enfant terrible* (bad boy) of French fashion.

Gaultier creates fashions that parody (rather than promote) the fashion establishment. His clothes seem to challenge the fashion world not to take itself so seriously. His collections have a pop-culture focus and manage somehow to be both formal and playful.

Jean Paul Gaultier likes to break the rules. In the '80s he started putting underwear on the outside of his designs. He designed Madonna's black studded bra that she wore for her Blonde Ambition tour in 1990. I would say this guy epitomizes kitsch!

I would have been happy to double my money on this $5 purchase, but was very pleasantly surprised when it got six bids and sold for $27! Kitschy! Put that in your title and smoke it. That's derived from "Put that in your pipe and smoke it," a phrase my grandmother used to say but that I never quite understood. I just learned that it is an impolite way of telling someone that they must accept what you have just said even if they do not like it. But I am certain that you liked learning more about kitsch!

# #38 C Jere owl

$5.00
**Paid**
From: Thrift store

## C. Curtis Jere Owl Mod Eames Sculpture Awesome!

### Description:
Signed Jere Owl is very modern and awesome! This piece is super. It does need some TLC. Signed on the back with C. Jere '68 (for 1968). Very mid-century modern and abstract. It is 12" by 7½" by 16". A very substantial piece. It is metal that has been decorated with some pieces of enamel or other similar medium. Part of this gold décor has come off. Mostly missing from the top of his head. The previous owner saved quite a few pieces-so hopefully it can be restored. It will be an amazing piece of Jere craftsmanship when professionally put back together.

**Winning Bid:**

$81.00

**Ended:** 10/29/05
**History:** 3 bids
**Starting Bid:** $9.99
**Winner:** New York, NY

**Viewed**
 X

## The Story

My mom and I stopped by my thrift store (well, I call it "mine" because it is my favorite one in town) one Saturday after garage saling. I walked in and immediately spotted this huge owl sculpture. He was marked "$5 'As Is' 10-22-05" (which means he had just been put out that morning) and I had a feeling about him.

I quickly purchased him and my mom and I headed out to her minivan. I started examining him and was excited to find a C. Jere '68 signature on the back side in black marker. My mom said "Get out! No way—that is not fair."

You see, my mom loves C. Jere pieces and has known about C. Jere since the 1960s. Whenever we find a unique metal piece from that era, we always quickly look for the black marker signature of C. Jere. These pieces can be worth a small fortune. C. Jere is known for huge wall sculptures, metal figural pieces and many other types of three-dimensional metal art.

I had always thought that Curtis Jere was one man. Turns out he never existed. Curtis Jere is a compound nom-de-plume (pen name) for a design group created at Artisan House in the 1960s. Artisan House is a Los Angeles-based studio formed by Jerry Fels (design and sales) and Curtis Freiler (production)—hence the business name Curtis Jere.

These two men no longer own Artisan House, but it is still in existence. The vintage (1960s to 1970s) hand-signed C. Jere pieces are the ones that sell for real money on eBay.

It turns out that many different artists contributed designs that were produced under the C. Jere name. Today, the C. Jere trademark is still being used by artists who create their sculptures under the direction of an Artisan House "Studio Master."

So I rushed home with my owl and listed him that morning on eBay. Just like when I was a kid and I rushed from ride to ride at Disneyland with my mom, time is of the essence. You never know what good things await you! So, whenever I get something really neat on a Saturday morning I will try to list it immediately. That owl had just been put into the thrift store that Saturday morning at 10 a.m. I bought him at 10:10 a.m. and he was listed on eBay by 10:59 a m — a l l within an hour. I love

immediate gratification! It was even better exactly one week later when he sold for $81—even in very "as is" condition!

# #39  EAPG Toothpick Holder

$5.<sup>00</sup>

**Paid**

**From:** Thrift store

**EAPG Toothpick Holder Etched Riverside Glass Empress**

**Description:**
This EAPG toothpick holder is antique.  Measures 2¾" by 2⅛".
Etched with flowers and leaves.  No gold clear Early American Pattern Glass (EAPG) circa 1899.  No chips no cracks no crazing.  Empress clear was made by the Riverside Glass Work.  I am guessing that the etching was added later.

**Winning Bid:**

# $102.<sup>50</sup>

**Ended:** 10/31/05
**History:** 7 bids
**Starting Bid:** $9.99
**Winner:** Ritzville, WA

**Viewed**

000087 **X**

# EAPG Toothpick Holder  #39

## The Story

I bought this piece at my thrift store on the same Saturday morning that I bought the Jere owl. It was priced at $5 and the tag also said "10/17 Pressed Glass Identified As: Riverside Glass Work/Empress Clear." So it had been sitting there for five days when I scooped it up.

You will hear me complain about the new-fangled thrift stores quite a bit. They are getting too smart for their own good and doing too much research. What happened to the old days when they would price things off the cuff (with no great thought)?

Now they are looking things up on eBay, printing out price sheets from Replacements and overall getting too big for their britches. Some of them are pricing like they are upper-end antiques stores. I hate to tell them that they are NOT and they are alienating their best customers—dealers like you and me—who are just trying to make an honest living.

OK, I will get down off my soapbox for now...So, even though they are doing research that typically hurts us—in this instance their research actually helped me!

I will always take a chance on a $5 piece of EAPG (which stands for Early American Pattern Glass). EAPG was the precursor to our modern tableware/dinnerware. It is what early Americans ate from and decorated their tables with.

Toothpick holders were used for just that—holding toothpicks. How fun to have a piece of tableware with a specific purpose like holding toothpicks? There are collectors for toothpick holders and for specific EAPG patterns. This pattern was identified for me as Empress—now *that* was worth the $5 purchase price in and of itself.

Riverside Glass Works operated from 1879 to 1907 (just 30 short years) in Wellsburg, West Virginia. The Empress pattern was made around the turn of the century, in 1898. An empress is the wife of an emperor or a female ruler—she could also be known as a queen. This pattern was made in crystal, emerald green and the very rare amethyst. Typically, colored pieces sell for the most money.

Speaking of the turn of the century, 1898, my daughter was born at the turn of this century, exactly 100 years later, in 1998.

I was able to list this piece quickly because of the help from the thrift store and I started the bidding at $9.99. What did I have to lose? Nothing. I ascertained that the etching was added later and this piece sold for $102.50 on Halloween day. I was thrilled!

It turns out that the toothpick holder in the Empress pattern is quite hard to find. Can you imagine what one in amethyst would be worth? Priceless—just like my daughter—a mini-empress and often a princess—and that is exactly what she was for Halloween in 2005.

# #40 Running Free Dinnerware

**$7.00** Paid
From: Thrift store

**Running Free Sailboats Noritake B968 1 Dinner Plate HTF**

**Description:**
Running Free sailboats dinner plate is very hard to find and expensive. In fact, the entire pattern is hard to find and we have quite a few pieces up for sale this week in separate auctions. This piece has slight utensil wear. It also has a tiny pinpoint spot on the edge that is missing the glaze. No real chips, no cracks no crazing. In good to very good condition. Style B968 by Noritake stoneware Primastone. The pattern is Running Free and is blue sailboats with blue band and trim. Very stylized and expensive.

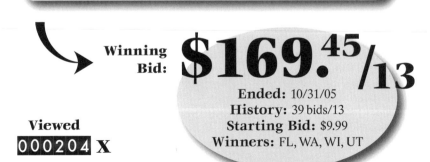

**Winning Bid:** **$169.**<sup>45</sup>/13

**Ended:** 10/31/05
**History:** 39 bids/13
**Starting Bid:** $9.99
**Winners:** FL, WA, WI, UT

**Viewed**
000204 X

# Running Free Dinnerware  #40

## The Story

One thing I have learned recently is that thrift stores don't know everything. Thank goodness! They also don't have the time to look up every single item they sell. With dinnerware sets, I think that they only research the name brands that they think are good, such as Lenox, Haviland, and Spode.

They often overlook brand names like Studio Nova, Gibson, and Mikasa (which can be great, depending on the pattern), and they almost always overlook stoneware, focusing instead on fine china. That is why this charming stoneware set from Noritake was only priced at $7. No one did any research. Yippppeeee!

When I got home with my little box of stoneware (four dinner plates, six salad plates, two cups, four saucers and four bowls) I was thrilled to see the prices listed on Replacements. com. The dinner plates alone listed for $49.99 each. My box added up to $579 at the retail prices posted. What a score for only $7!

I was especially drawn to this sailboat set because I had just finished teaching one of my first six-week ecourses. At the end, I have all my students join a teleseminar to discuss what they have learned. When one of my students, Janet King, got on the line, she said, "It is martini time here in New York." I immediately liked her! She told us about a needlepoint belt with sailboats that she had bought for $1 at a tag sale. She had it up for sale in an auction that was going to end that night—and it was already up to $60.

Janet had a hunch about the needlepoint belt because she lives on the East Coast where the America's Cup, and sailing gener-

ally, are very popular. The America's Cup is the most famous and prestigious regatta in sailing. It is known as the "Holy Grail" of sailing, and in recent years, it seems that the sailboats themselves—their technology and the science behind their designs—have become even more important than the skills of the crews who sail them.

Well, the next morning I couldn't wait to see where Janet's belt had ended up. I checked her completed auctions and was astonished to see that it had sold for over $200! I immediately emailed her a congratulations and she told me that my note was the first she knew about it selling for so much. Now, that is what you call a "Holy Grail" of a belt!

Sailing is a huge American pastime and items with sailboats tend to do well—another reason I scooped up this set for only $7. I was super happy when the pieces sold for $169.45 in thirteen separate auctions. I typically get about 30% of Replacements prices when I sell on eBay; 30% of the Replacements.com total of $579 is $173.70—only $4.25 off of my total sale price. Now, that is what I call science—science of the eBay variety!

# #41  Bonsai Tree

**Bonsai Tree Brass Copper Bronze Sculpture 1970s Vintage**

**Description:**

Bonsai tree is vintage and very heavy. It is some type of metal. Brass, copper, or bronze? Needs cleaning and/or polishing. In very good condition. 8.5" by 6". Originally used as a golf trophy but these added features could be removed. Says "Cat's Paw Invitational" and there is a golf flag.

**Winning Bid:**

# $83.89

**Ended:** 10/31/05
**History:** 15 bids
**Starting Bid:** $9.99
**Winner:** Lafayette, CA

**Viewed**
000269 X

# Bonsai Tree  #41

## The Story

This story cracks me up. I am always telling people that bonsai in any shape or form sells. I don't care if it is plastic (I sold a throw-away plastic one for $15.49), ceramic, porcelain, stone, or metal—it will sell!

Bonsai is the art of growing carefully trained dwarf plants in containers. The literal translation of the Japanese word is "tree in a tray." The idea behind this ancient art form is to emulate nature by bringing it inside and pruning the trees in such a way that they give the illusion of age.

So, I bought this "bonsai" at a garage sale for $2. It was a trophy from a 1975 golf tournament. I figured that the golf plaquette could be removed and the new owner would have a lovely "bonsai" metal sculpture.

Well, I am obviously not too bright, because if you look at this piece closely, you will see that the tree is huge. It towers over the tiny golf hole and flag. It is in no sense of the word a "bonsai," but I didn't find this out until the nice new owner emailed me.

Turns out that Danny Garcia is still active in the art world and has owned his gallery in Carmel, California, since 1959. He is believed to hold the record for the longest continuously run gallery in Carmel.

I would bet that my grandmother also holds the record for the longest continuously run antique store in Bellingham, WA. She was in business for 52 years and that will be hard to beat!

Back to Danny. He is also well known for his interesting sculptures of trees (like mine) and if you look on the back cover of Bill Clinton's autobiography, you will see one sitting on the desk in the Oval office—a gift from Clinton Chief of Staff (and Garcia fan) Leon Panetta. Wow! Pretty cool.

A cypress tree! Yikes! How did Rick ever find my auction? I am sure glad he did, because this piece ended up selling for $83.89. Just goes to show you, that even with a huge mistake in the title like this—things can still sell for big bucks!

Hi Lynn, I would love to be included in your book. I, of course, still have the tree sculpture. It is one of my favorite pieces of art. I believe it to be a very early piece by Danny Garcia of Carmel, California. I hope he is still with us. I know his health was poor the last time we saw he and his wife. They sell mostly cypress tree sculptures that are very free-form, and no two are alike. Thank you again.
-Rick Wadman

Garcia Tre

Front- and spine-of-cover photograph: Bob McNeely
Back-of-cover photographs courtesy of
the Clinton Presidential Materials Project
Cover design by Carol Devine Carson

U.S. $17.95    Can. $23.95
ISBN 1-4000-3003-X

5 1 7 9 5

# #42 Nadalin Skateboard

**$3.00** Paid
From: Garage sale

## Speed Spring Skateboard Vintage Ed Nadalin CA 1980s

**Description:**
Speed Springs skateboard says "Nadalin" on the top. I couldn't find out any information about this board. It says "Speed Spring" on the wheels/springs and what looks like "Nadalin" on the top. For Ed Nadalin, who was a local Irvine skateboarder? 23.5" by 5.75". In used condition. I am guessing the 1970s to 1980s.

**Winning Bid:** **$103.**$^{51}$

**Ended:** 11/3/05
**History:** 13 bids
**Starting Bid:** $9.99
**Winner:** Oxfordshire, UK

**Viewed**
000122 X

# Nadalin Skateboard  #42

## The Story

I keep buying skateboards and they never sell. I have two in my eBay office right now that I keep tripping on. That could be a huge cartoon-style disaster! I keep hoping I will find a skateboard that is super-rare and sells for a small fortune.

Well, this one is my first skateboard success story! I think the key is to buy the skinny boards, not the fat ones. But who really knows? Not me—I am no skateboard expert.

I found this skateboard on the ground at a garage sale and paid $3 for it. I couldn't quite figure out what it said, but I came up with "Nadalin." Turns out that Ed Nadalin is a famous skateboarder from Orange County, and he was nice enough to help me out with writing this story!

Ed was one of the best freestyle skaters in the mid 1970s. He often skated at the Huntington Beach Pier. Freestyle is now considered "old school" in opposition to the "new school" street style. Old school freestyle was always done on flat ground and had five main categories: footwork, spins, handstands, aerials, and multiple board tricks.

Ed was the featured skater in "The Magic Rolling Board," a fourteen-minute video that you can still view on Google. I just watched it, and it was a trip to see Ed in 1976 dancing on his skateboard wearing an all-white tuxedo. The "old school" freestyle is a lot of fun to watch. I can see why Ed gained the nickname "Mr. Fluidity."

Ed and another famous California skater, Russ Howell, endorsed the skateboard that I was selling on eBay for the Power Paw Speed Spring Company. Ed tells me that they were never compensated for the marketing of the boards or for the R & D (research and development) that they did for the trucks. Bummer!

The trucks are the metal pieces that hold the wheels. Ed tells me that the Speed Spring trucks were incredible for freestyle, but failed at anything else. "But that was what we did—freestyle, flatground, we didn't need anything else back in the 1970s."

Unfortunately, freestyle was soon left behind. Russ Howell says, "The skate magazines don't promote flatland freestyle because they see no profit in it. Many of the freestylists left the sport during the late '70s because their sponsors saw no money in keeping them active. Only a handful were able to make a transition to the 'new school' form. But I still get a lot of request to teach 'old school' freestyle to other skaters at the skatepark."

In the meantime, Ed Nadalin (whose endorsement was on my board) lives in Italy and works in the film industry. He writes, "I really don't do much skateboarding anymore." How sad! I hope that maybe freestyle flatland skating will experience a rebirth. In any case, this very cool skateboard sold for over $100 (plus another $37 in shipping) and ended up being mailed to the U.K.—close to "Mr. Fluidity," now living in Rome.

# #43  Wilton Pewter Chargers

**$15.00**
Paid
From: Garage sale

## Wilton Armetale 3 Pewter Dinner Plates Federal ? Plow

**Description:**

3 Pewter Wilton Armetale Plates are 10⅞" in diameter. We have a lot of plates in this pattern up for sale this week. They are signed "Wilton Colombia PA USA" and "RWP." Also the plow backstamp. I thought these may be the Federal, Nathaniel Austin, or plow tavern pattern but none seem to match perfectly. Please let me know if you know. Thanks! These are in as-is to OK condition. They have a lot of utensil wear and marks. I don't know if these can be polished down—it would be worth a try.

**Winning Bid:** **$240.09/6**

**Ended:** 11/3/05
**History:** 54 bids/6
**Starting Bid:** $9.99 each
**Winners:** MA, NY

**Viewed**
000426 X

# Wilton Pewter Chargers  #43

## The Story

I first learned about Wilton Armetale through a wedding present from my great friend Juliette Capretta Baia. It was the most beautiful platter, huge and heavy—I still own it. She told me it was from a great company. Typical Capretta—of course it would be of the highest quality, and it was signed on the back "Wilton Armetale."

Capretta and I have been friends since sitting next to each other on an airplane going to Madrid in 1984. I actually disliked her at the start. She had huge poodle-type hair and an over-the-top personality.

I decided right away that we were not destined to be friends, but over the next five months that we spent together in Spain, I learned to love her. In fact, when we graduated from college in 1985, we became roommates in the Brentwood section of Los Angeles.

We ended up living together until 1991, when I bought a townhouse in the Valley. We were great roommates and went through a lot together. We got along really well. She was neat and clean and I wasn't. Felix and Oscar! She always joked to my ex-husband that he would be taking over the role of house cleaner! I still don't do house cleaning—I hire it out.

Anyway, Wilton Armetale is a family-owned and -operated business that was founded in 1892 by Ralph P. Wilton, Sr. in Lancaster County, Pennsylvania. An offshoot of the original company, The Wilton Brass Company, was established in 1954 and offered brass objects for sale. In 1963, this company developed a new metal from an aluminum-based alloy which it called "armetale."

By the late 1960s, armetale items outsold brass items, but the company continued to be known as the "Wilton Brass Company" until well into the 1980s. After that, items began being marked as "Wilton Armetale" with a plow logo and "Wilton Colombia PA" and "RWP" (the initials for Ralph P. Wilton).

Armetale is an aluminum-based alloy. It helps keep hot foods hot and cold foods cold. Every piece is handmade so no two pieces are exactly alike.

What I have learned is that Wilton Armetale pieces sell for big bucks on eBay! I saw this stack of Armetale chargers at a garage sale for $15. There were eighteen pieces total, so that made it less than $1 per piece. Sold!

I put them on eBay in six separate auctions of three chargers each, starting at $9.99 per auction. These plates were in as-is to okay condition, with lots of utensil marks and scratches. I made this very clear in the description.

I couldn't believe it when the six auctions brought in a total of $240.09. What a score. If these plates can sell for that much in "as is" condition, can you even imagine what they would have sold for in excellent condition? If only Capretta had been around to polish out the utensil marks for me—just kidding!

# #44 Cathrineholm Fondue

$2.00 Paid
From: Garage sale

**Norway Cathrineholm Eames Era Viking Fondue Kettle RARE**

### Description:

This is an amazing fondue piece in avocado green. Complete, mint set with the original brochure. There is one tiny tiny 1/16" round piece missing enamel on the inside of the lid—you can't even see it! Made in Norway, Cathrineholm Ltd. 9.5" by 11.5". Six pieces including the candle. Where will you find one of these in such pristine condition? The brochure says, "It's a fondue set, It's a soup tureen, It's a casserole. It's the new six-piece cooking set ideal on the patio or for a traveling picnic. Cook or heat with sterno or candle. Use the bowl for salad and the tray for serving. Magnificent enamel-ware with polished steel stand. $22.50" I would guess 1960s. What a find!

**Winning Bid:**

**$37.00**

**Ended:** 11/12/05
**History:** 7 bids
**Starting Bid:** $9.99
**Winner:** Japan

**Viewed**
000048 X

# Cathrineholm Fondue  #44

## The Story

This super-neat enamel set was at a community garage sale in Palm Desert and marked only $2. It was so awesome and in pristine condition. Every single piece was present and it even came with the original pamphlet.

The company was Cathrineholm (one word), and it was difficult to research. I originally thought that Cathrine Holm must have been a woman designer. I was wrong, but I did find out some interesting facts. Cathrineholm was the name of an old ironworks that was located by the end of a waterfall in Tistedal, Norway. Production started at this factory in 1907, and they made wrought iron, chains, nails and agriculture equipment.

My father's mother's family came from Lillehammer, Norway, and I am half Norwegian. My dad's mother's name was Hulda Agnes Johnson; she was born in 1897, ten years before this company was founded. She married in 1920 at the age of 23 and went on to have thirteen live-birth children. Yikes! She had her last baby at the age of 45 in 1942. Now that is a miracle! She was an amazing woman who had a master's degree in music and yet chose to raise thirteen children on a farm in South Dakota. Tistedal—where Cathrineholm was located—was only 188 miles from Lillehammer, her family's home.

As demand for the items produced in Tistedal waned and profitability dropped, they looked for other items to save the company. The answer came in the form of enamel-on-steel kitchen items.

Enamel consists of nearly the same raw material as china glaze, but it is much stronger because it has steel as a base instead of clay. Interesting!

Skilled workmen were imported from Germany and other countries. The factory eventually employed some top European designers, and many of the enamel pieces were designed by Grete Prytz Korsmo, the second wife of famed architect Arne Korsmo. These Cathrineholm pieces are the epitome of mid-century modern Eames era (1947 to 1969) pieces. No wonder they are so collectible.

The company enjoyed a heyday from 1930 to 1965. By 1970, kitchenware competition from stainless steel, aluminum and plastics was too strong, and the company had to shut down.

I hate to hear about any company shutting down, but many of these enamel pieces have found wonderful homes with collectors, so the legacy lives on—just as the legacy of my paternal grandmother lives on in the thirteen children she had, the 65 grandchildren she had (I am one of those—so many cousins that I hardly remember all their names) and the 110 great-grandchildren (Houston and Indiana have over a hundred second cousins.) Wow!

# #45  Silverplate Cow Lid

**Victorian Silverplate Figural Lid Bull Steer Cow Ornate**

## Description:

Victorian silverplate lid with a cow is quite ornate. This is the coolest lid for a butter dish. Ornate with etched leaves and a figural finial. 5.25" by 4" tall. In very good condition. May need replating. A neat piece; I would guess 1880s. We bought a lot of interesting silverplate items that will be up for sale in the next few weeks. Antique butter dishes, pickle castors etc. We didn't polish any of these items and instead will let the new buyers decide whether to polish or not. Please check out all of our auctions for more silverplate items.

**Winning Bid:**

# $72.<sup>98</sup>

**Ended:** 11/12/05
**History:** 9 bids
**Starting Bid:** $9.99
**Winner:** Flushing, MI

**Viewed**
000097 X

# Silverplate Cow Lid  #45

## The Story

My dad was visiting and he went to help me pick up some stuff that I had bought. My dad is always willing to help out. He grew up working on his family's farm and started milking cows when he was six years old. He has an incredible work ethic. When we arrived at the seller's home, it was the second day of her sale and she was putting out an entire table of silverplate parts.

What are silverplate parts? If a piece of silver is large and heavy, with ornate designs or engraving, it could be an 18th century or early 19th century piece. It may be sterling silver, but it is more likely to be Victorian silverplate. Victorian silverplate was made from either copper, nickel silver or a white metal called Britannia, which was then coated with a thin layer of real sterling silver. Silverplating was introduced in 1840, and inexpensive plated wares became available in quantity soon after.

Silverplated wares included pickle castor frames, butter dishes, spoon holders, brides basket frames and all sorts of fancy flatware. A lot of the silverplated items were designed to be coupled or matched with glass inserts.

What I have found over the years is that silverplated parts can do very well on their own, without the glass inserts—infact, sometimes the parts sell for more than a complete piece. So I asked the lady, how much for the entire table? Well, her niece was there, and the niece did not want her aunt to sell anything. The niece started grabbing items that she wanted for herself.

The lady holding the sale told me to wait outside as she rolled her eyes. She said it was always tough with family, but that she wanted to sell the entire bunch of stuff and would make me a great deal. She took the niece inside and came back to talk turkey with me. She said, "How about $75 for everything?" There were about 35 pieces, and that sounded more than fair.

My dad and I boxed it all up and it barely fit in my car with all the other things I was taking home that day. It was quite a challenge. In fact, my car bottomed out when we pulled out of the driveway. Always a sign of a major score! This lid was in with all those silverplated items.

I put it on eBay with "Victorian" in the title. Keep in mind that this was just a lid, and the silverplating was very worn. I couldn't believe it when it ended up selling for $72.98! This one little piece almost paid for the entire table full! I think it sold for so much because anything with animals does very well. I wonder if the cow that they used as a model was one of the ones that my dad used to milk on the farm in South Dakota? Probably not!

# #46 Enid Collins LOVE Box Bag

**$0.<sup>00</sup> Paid**

**From:** Gift with a purchase

**Enid Collins Original Box Bag Love Texas Vintage NEAT!**

### Description:

Enid Collins box bag is from Texas and very neat. Collins of Texas. 8.5" by 4" by 5.5". It says "Love" in green – pink and greens on a light wood base. Very 1960s to 1970s. It is so cute. Slight wear. It needs a cleaning. There is one stone missing and three of the little daisies are missing one petal. The paint still looks in great shape. Has an "EC" handpainted on the top. Great purse! Mod op art!

**Winning Bid:**

**$67.<sup>00</sup>**

**Ended:** 11/14/05
**History:** 15 bids
**Starting Bid:** $9.99
**Winner:** Huntington Beach, CA

**Viewed**
000122 X

# Enid Collins LOVE Box Bag   #46

## The Story

At the sale where I bought all the silverplate, I met a friend of the lady running the sale who said she had a set of dishes to sell. I made arrangements to go by and see the dishes the next day.

The dishes were nice, and she wanted $75 for them. I bought them, and as I was leaving she said that she wanted to give me this purse. She didn't want any money for it, she just wanted it gone.

It was signed with "EC" on the outside and "Collins of Texas" on the inside. It was very mod op art and was marked "Love" on the top. It turns out that "EC" stands for Enid Roessler Collins, who was famous for her Enid Collins of Texas purses—those cute, kitschy (please see story #37), sequined, sprinkled, jeweled-covered purses of the 1960s.

Enid grew up in San Antonio Texas. She attended Texas Women's University in the 1940s, where she majored in fashion design. She married Frederic Collins and they moved to a ranch outside of Media. Enid began doing what she loved. She followed her passion (just like my grandma did and I do today) of combining art and fashion, and in doing so she created one of the most recognizable purses of the retro-craze vintage era. Enid Collins bags were much beloved. According to the research I did, "You knew you were all grown up when your mother let you spend money on an Enid Collins purse."

Enid and her husband started out in 1959 by designing each purse with handpainting and personal art work. They used silk screening, imported crystal cut gemstones, seed pearls, paint and gemstones. But soon (in 1968), a factory was built, and purses were manufactured by the thousands. From 1966 to 1968, Enid and her husband also manufactured papier mache purses at a factory in Puerto Rico, and it is these that are the most coveted.

Her two main styles of purses were the wood mahogany box bag and the canvas bucket bag. Her whimsical designs drew from the Texas landscape and surrounding wildlife. The purses were covered with roadrunners, lady bugs, peacocks and horses. Some of the purses even had whimsical and colorful sayings. The purses each had a theme, and some of these were the zodiac, owls, kittens, partridges in pear trees, and "under the sea."

An important thing to remember is that all her original pre-1968 purses were signed and dated with a small "ec" and possibly the copyright mark ("c") and the date. Later purses were signed differently. In 1970, the Tandy leather company bought her out and started marking the bags with a capital "C" or "Collins of Texas" with a running horse.

All good things eventually end—which is too bad. The Tandy company stopped producing her purses in the late 1970s, and now to make a young girl's eyes sparkle and her heart skip a beat over an Enid Collin bag you will have to buy it for her on eBay. My free bag sold for over $60! The dinnerware set I bought barely sold, but just like Enid Collins, I am fortunate to be able to do what I LOVE every day—find treasures to sell on eBay!

# #47 Sinking of the Titanic Book

$0.<sup>17</sup>

**Paid**

**From:** Garage sale

## Memorial Edition Sinking of Titanic Minter 1912 Stories

### Description:

This memorial edition of the Titanic story includes thrilling stories told by survivors. Name and a price are written in the front. 6.5" by 9". Blue boards with photo of the ship. Minter Harrisburg 1912. List of passengers and photos. 287 pages. In "as is" condition. All the pages are intact and it is readable. A very interesting book. I bought an extensive collection of antique and classic books—well over 600. I will try and get them all listed quickly. Please ask all questions early so that we can get them answered before bidding ends. Don't miss out—we have some really wonderful and rare books up for auction.

**Winning Bid:**

# $51.<sup>00</sup>

**Ended:** 11/14/05
**History:** 10 bids
**Starting Bid:** $9.99
**Winner:** Columbus, Ohio

**Viewed**
000088 X

# Sinking of the Titanic Book  #47

## The Story

It is a rare Friday when my mom and I go out garage saling. We do not like Fridays because we never seem to find anything and it can waste two to three hours of our workday. But when we see an estate sale advertised in Rancho Mirage we will go. Why? Rancho Mirage is nicknamed "the playground of the presidents"—Gerald Ford and Eisenhower had homes there. It is worth a Friday trip.

We walked into the house and were told that the man of the house had passed away. His wife was running the sale and she showed us his book collection. There were at least 600, if not 800, books. You know me—or you should be beginning to know me. I asked, "How much for all of them?" She said $100. Sold.

That was less than seventeen cents each. Score! I know nothing about books—it is not my area of expertise—but at seventeen cents a book, what did I have to lose?

My dad was still in town, so after my mom and I hauled all the books home, I put him right to work. He was a librarian in a past life—before he retired—so I had him sort all the books by subject. There were golf, baseball, Mark Twain, gambling, history, and art books. It was really quite a nice collection. I decided to put all the Mark Twain books and some of the history books up for auction right away.

The Mark Twain books didn't sell at auction, but I will tell you this. They have almost all now sold for $9.99 each out of my eBay store. I am not kidding—it is so awesome. Books will eventually sell if you let them sit in your store long enough.

This Titanic book was one of the history books that I listed that first week. I have always been fascinated with the Titanic and its history. The Titanic sank the year my grandmother was born. The Titanic was launched on the 31st of May, 1911, but was never christened before it sunk on Sunday evening, April 14th, 1912, at 11:40 pm. Cheryl Leaf was only three months old.

There were 2,208 passengers, with 324 in first class, 285 in second class, 708 in third class and 891 crew members. It was so opulent that the second and third class cabins were said to be just as fancy as the first class cabins on other boats. Estimates put the number of dead at 1,500 and the survivors at around 700 because (as you probably know) there were only twenty lifeboats. The sinking of the Titanic is known as one of the worst peacetime maritime disasters of all time.

The last movie that I took my grandmother to see in a theater was James Cameron's *Titanic*. It was January of 1998, and my ex-husband and I took her for her birthday. We sat in the back of the theater in the handicapped section and she loved the film. She would always tear up over television shows, movies and even the news! She was very emotional, and she sure cried that day. Whenever she would start blubbering, I would ask, "Are you crying?" and she would always say "NO!" I do the same thing when my kids ask me!

No wonder this book in as-is condition sold for over $50 and paid for half my collection of 600 books. And I got to remember a special day with my grandma.

# #48  Jim Beam Bulldog Decanter

$3.<sup>50</sup>

**Paid**

**From:** Garage sale

**Jim Beam Decanter Marines Devil Dog Bulldog HTF Vintage**

**Description:**
Jim Beam Decanter is vintage. Says "DEVIL DOGS" on his hat. This one is hard to find. It is in excellent condition but needs cleaning. 10" by 5".

**Winning Bid:**

# $80.<sup>00</sup>

**Ended:** 11/17/05
**History:** 10 bids
**Starting Bid:** $9.99
**Winner:** Grovetown, GA

**Viewed**
000110 X

# Jim Beam Bulldog Decanter #48

## The Story

Don't you see whiskey decanters everywhere? I do. And more often than not they are priced way too high. It is like the Avon bottle curse—now we have the Jim Beam curse. People who inherit or have collected whiskey decanters seem to believe that these items are worth a small fortune.

I am not sure why I bought this Jim Beam decanter on a Saturday morning in November. I think the reason was that it featured a bulldog, and bulldog collectors are crazy. I have since learned that some Jim Beam decanters will bring big bucks on eBay.

The Jim Beam company was established in 1795, and not only produces fine whiskey but also designs artistic containers for whiskey. I am not a whiskey drinker, but I found it really interesting that there have been seven generations of Beam family members dating back to 1795 who have distilled for the company. They have kept it a real family business, just like Cheryl Leaf Antiques.

I made a big commitment to my grandmother and her business when I moved home in 1993 to take over. I not only ran the shop, but I also took care of her. Her health was failing and I became her main caregiver. I learned all about transfer boards, wheelchairs, walkers, and the trapeze. I also learned what home healthcare and taking care of our elderly really requires. It is not for the weak-spirited. I feel compassion for anyone that

has ever gone through what we went through. My grandmother deserved every second of my time, and luckily, she appreciated each and every moment I spent with her. She was a wonderful woman.

I have tried to infuse her spirit into my eBay business and the books I write to keep the tradition going that was started back in 1950 in that little house at the corner of Northwest and Illinois in Bellingham, Washington.

It was in 1952, just two years after my grandmother opened her store, that Beam introduced their specialty bottles, making a distinct change from their conventional whiskey bottles.

The first specialty bottle introduced was a glass cocktail shaker. In 1957, the first of the famous trophy bottles were issued. During the following years, in answer to the growing demand for these bottles, Beam issued both china and glass decanters, each unique in conception and design. There were sports (horse racing, football), wheels, trophies, ducks and many other series produced. Most collectors focus on specific series.

The Jim Beam bottles that sell for the most are the ones given as awards to their salespeople. There are several other whiskey companies (such as Ezra Brooks) that have entered the decanter market, but the Jim Beam decanters are the best—just like Cheryl Leaf and Cheryl Leaf Antiques.

# #49 Weiss Christmas Pin Brooch

$2.00
**Paid**
**From:** Church sale

## Weiss Vintage Rhinestone Christmas Tree Pin Brooch Eames

### Description:

Weiss vintage rhinestone pin is very Eames era. I am guessing that this beautiful pin is from the 1950s Eames era. Signed "Weiss" on the back. 2¾" by 1¾". In very good to excellent condition. Light and dark green rhinestones make up the tree, 6 clear white candles, larger red rhinestones and the base is amber rhinestones. Super piece.

**Winning Bid:** $152.50

**Ended:** 11/19/05
**History:** 10 bids
**Starting Bid:** $9.99
**Winner:** Englewood, FL

**Viewed**
000182 X

# Weiss Christmas Pin Brooch  #49

## The Story

On a Saturday morning in November, at 5:55 am, the door to my bedroom opened and in stepped my six-year-old daughter, Indiana. Clutching her clothes in one hand, she said, "Mommy, I am going to garage sales with you today." I asked, "Why?" She said, "Because it is fun and I want to spend time with you and Mor Mor" (Swedish for "mother's mother," which is what my kids call their grandmother). How could I say no to that?

So, at 6:45 am, off we went, three generations of antique dealers. My grandmother would have been so proud to see us all carrying on her tradition.

Indy had $5 of her own money to spend, and she ended up getting some Christmas presents and a few knick-knacks for her room. At one sale, a woman was selling Christmas cards. Indiana is very serious when she shops, and she finally decided on a "Dear Mommy" card and parted with 50 cents for it. That was so sweet—it made me want to cry!

There was a sale at the Armenian church that was scheduled to start at 11 am. It was only listed in the *Penny Saver* and not in the newspaper, so we thought there was a good chance it wouldn't be crowded. There were signs and balloons all over advertising the

sale, but the signs had no start time listed. It was only 10:30 am, but we decided to go by early. I typically don't do this; I am a rule follower, not a rule breaker!

However, we went. The doors were open and there were a lot of people inside, so we started shopping. One lady

asked, "Do you work for the church?" and we said, "No, we are here for your sale." She said, "Oh, no! It doesn't start for half an hour." I replied, "We saw all sorts of signs with no time listed" and she said, "Fine."

I was all done shopping and Indiana was looking at the jewelry table. She picked up a Christmas tree pin (she loves Christmas because her birthday is in December) and showed it to me. It was signed "Weiss" and only marked $2, so I decided to buy it.

Weiss was founded in 1942 by Albert Weiss, a former Coro employee. The company offered high-quality costume jewelry, including Christmas tree pins made for Weiss in Germany. The company closed its doors in 1971.

We got home and I researched the pin and found one exactly like it on eBay that had sold for $86! Wow—what a score! I told Indiana that I would give her 20% of its selling price as a finder's fee. We had so much fun watching this auction together, and the pin ended up selling for $152.50! Amazing.

I paid Indy $30.50. She is now hooked on eBay and wants to go garage saling with us every weekend. As an end note, I think our pin sold for double the price of the other one for several reasons. I put "brooch" in the title, and the other seller only used "pin." I also put "Eames" in the title and (once again), that is a very searchable term. Finally, it was the perfect time of year to sell a Christmas tree pin that my daughter's bright eyes spotted!

# #50  Stuart Abelman Vase

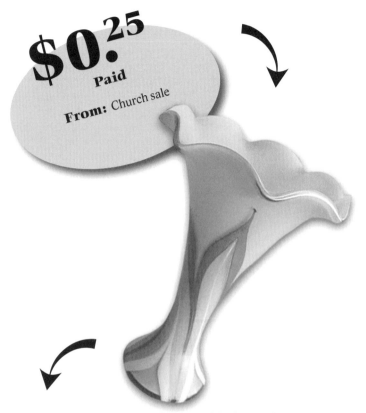

$0.$^{25}$
**Paid**
**From:** Church sale

**Stuart Abelman Art Glass Pulled Feather 1980 Vase RARE**

## Description:

Stuart Abelman art glass vase is very rare and beautiful. It is lavender/light blue base color and has other shades of blue and in the light the pulled feathers appear to be turquoise or sky blue. Vintage from the 1980s. Signed "V-100-21 1980 Ableman." 8" by 5½" by 3". In very good to excellent condition. No chips no cracks. Hard to find ruffled vase.

**Winning Bid:**

# $122.$^{26}$

**Ended:** 11/19/05
**History:** 8 bids
**Starting Bid:** $9.99
**Winner:** Boulder Creek, CA

**Viewed**
000188 X

# Stuart Abelman Vase   #50

## The Story

Before Indy found the Weiss pin, I had made a pile of stuff at that Armenian Church charity sale. I found some great things and my pile was pretty huge. My mom walked by this heap of items and thought to herself, "Oh, no, someone beat us to all the great stuff!" We laughed about it later because it was mine!

In that pile was this amazingly beautiful vase. It was a pulled feather design and looked like a piece of art glass. It was also signed, and the best part—it was only marked 25 cents. What a bargain!

When I got it home, I was thrilled to be able to read the signature. This is always a challenge, because even though a piece may be signed, if you can't read the signature, you have a problem. This vase was signed "1980 Abelman." You may remember Stuart Abelman from story #58 in my second *100 Best Things* book.

I listed this on eBay at 1:53 pm on the Saturday afternoon that I was going to a concert with my mom. Out here in Palm Desert we have a lot of great opportunities. Right up the road from my house is the Indian Wells Tennis Gardens. Every year, a world class tennis event is played there in March. During the off season, the tennis facility has started holding concerts.

On that Saturday night it was going to be an Eagles concert. I think at least t w o m e m - b e r s

of the Eagles, Don Henley and Glenn Fry, have homes out here. I grew up listening to my mom playing her favorite records (yes—no CD's back then) and her favorites were the Eagles, John Denver, Chicago, and Hamilton Joe, Frank & Reynolds ("Baby, baby 'fawin' in love. I'm 'fawin' in love again"). I can still picture her when we lived upstairs at my grandma's in 1977 while our house was being built. She would be sewing late at night and cranking the tunes.

So, we thought it would be a riot to go and hear the Eagles. We had pretty good seats and the concert was really awesome. While we were there, this vase was already getting some bids!

Stuart Abelman's glass studio was founded in 1977 in Van Nuys, California—the same year I was listening to the Eagles above the antique store. My vase was made in 1980, so it was one of his very early pieces. Watch for Ableman's clowns and frogs—these typically command more money than his paperweights and vases.

It was also in 1977 that the Eagles' "Hotel California" hit #1 in the U.S. Oddly enough, while I was at that Eagles concert, this 25-cent vase was already on its way to hitting #1 for me and selling for $122.26—489 times the purchase price! That may be my best return ever, and it was wonderful seeing the Eagles return to play here in California!

# #51 Raub Totem Pole

**$3.⁰⁰** Paid

**From:** Estate sale

## Stacey Raub Totem Pole Native American Makah NEAT Ed

**Description:**
Signed "Stacey Raub," totem pole is very neat. Could Stacey be related to Ed Raub? This model-sized totem pole is black, green, red and natural wood. It is very nice. Measures 11⅝" by 2¼". I would imagine that Stacey is a relative of the famous Skokomish/Makah Indian carver Ed Raub. In great condition.

**Winning Bid:**

**$40.⁹⁹**

**Ended:** 11/22/05
**History:** 8 bids
**Starting Bid:** $9.99
**Winner:** Las Vegas, NV

**Viewed**
**000067 X**

# Raub Totem Pole  #51

## The Story

I love history—especially family history. I used to spend hours sitting with my grandmother going through family photo albums, listening as she told me about the people in the pictures.

She would also patiently show us the few family items in her treasure-filled cabinets. Family was always very important to my grandmother, perhaps because she lost her mother when she was only fifteen months old. What a tragedy.

Totems are used to preserve family histories. This totem pole was hand-carved and signed "Stacey Raub." I learned that he was a famous model totem pole carver from the Makah tribe, who live on the Olympic peninsula in Washington state.

My grandmother's family left Illinois to live in Washington state after her mother, Maybelle, died in 1913.

Maybelle left very few physical items for her children. My grandmother, the pack rat, carried those items around with her for her entire life. They were her last and only ties to a mother she never knew.

I am very fortunate that my grandmother gave those items to me. I have the etched drinking glass that says "Toots" (Maybelle's nickname), her sterling spoon, and two of the pictures she painted—one when she was only eighteen. They are incredible.

I also have the gold watch that her father Peter S. Nelson gave to her, engraved "Maybellle from Papa May 3rd 1899." The watch was a gift for her 21st birthday, and Maybelle's husband George placed her picture in the watch after her death and carried it around in his breast pocket for years.

Here is an excerpt from a letter written to my grandmother from her father right after Maybelle died in April 1913: "My dear little Cheryl, you are too small to understand this, but I want you to read it when you are a big girl going to school. It's too bad that your good Mama was taken from us at so early an age. She loved you and Houston so much, but she's gone to Heaven and we will all see her and have a great family reunion in the land that knows no pain. Love and Kisses from your Papa."

In September of 1924, George sent another letter to my grandmother. "Dear Cheryl, It seems funny to be writing to you at Chicago—in fact it reminds me of when I used to write to your mother there, which has been almost 20 years ago. My, how times flies and you are almost a young lady and a mighty good one too. I could write you a book telling you all about what a good girl your mother was, but it makes the tears come. Bushels of Love from 'Dad Old Kid' (the name you gave me)."

Tragic that all that is left of Maybelle's short life is just five objects, a few letters, and photos. But I am grateful that Maybelle's incredible spirit and love of life were carried on within my grandmother, who was able to share them with me during my life.

I think that when Stacey Raub carves his incredible small totem poles, he wants to share the heritage of his family and his tribe—their spirit—with others. No wonder the totem pole sold for over $40.

# #52 Panton Desk Organizer

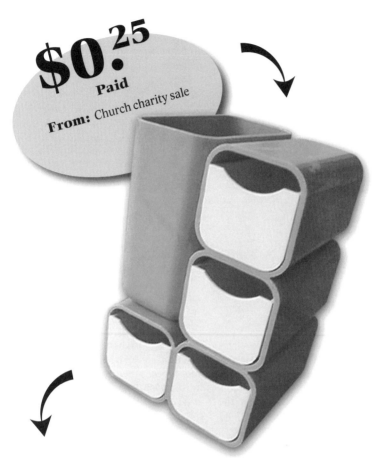

## Green Plastic Desk Organizer Panton Eames Space Age

**Description:**
Green plastic desk organizer is a small item with drawers. Needs cleaning and there are some pen marks in the base. Also a 1" split in the side. 3" by 3" by 4⅝" and very mid-century modern.

**Winning Bid:**

**$12.⁵¹**

**Ended:** 11/30/05
**History:** 4 bids
**Starting Bid:** $9.99
**Winner:** Kutztown, PA

**Viewed**
000029 X

# Panton Desk Organizer #52

## The Story

It was right after Thanksgiving, and I had finally sent the corrected manuscript of the Wiley book to the publishers. It felt as if it had taken me all year to write that book, and I spent my Thanksgiving doing a final read-through!

I got into trouble with *The Unofficial Guide* because I decided that a lot of pictures would make it a better book. I think my advance was about $6,500 (book advances are not as large as they used to be), and I had to pay my brother to do all the graphics and photos. To make sure we were on the right track, we had sent a sample first chapter to Wiley, and they had signed off on the number of photos and the specs.

My brother and I are a great team, and I was about $2,500 into him for his work when the editors finally started getting chapters back to me with their edits. They slashed almost 60% of my photos. Then they told us that the photos we had sent in didn't meet their specs, and I had to pay my brother to redo them. It was one of those grin and bear it moments in my life.

So, I was thrilled to have all of that behind me, and I was ready to celebrate the season! I picked up this little desk piece for only 25 cents. My mom had owned the exact same piece in orange, and it always sat on a desk in our family room. Remember, you should purchase anything that reminds you of your childhood!

I listed this on eBay with "Panton" in the title. My research had shown me that a Dane named Verner Panton might have been the designer. Verner was born in 1926 in a tiny village; he wanted to become an artist, but showed no real talent, so he eventually became an architecture student.

During the "beat" years of the mid-1950s, Panton bought a battered old camper for traveling across the continent. He had it customized into a mobile studio. Every few months he would trek across Europe to drop in on fellow designers and manufacturers in the hopes that they would buy his work. Panton's passion was for plastics and other man-made materials; he used them to create the vibrant colors in his geometric pop art.

He eventually came to be known as a visionary designer, in large part because of his "Panton chair"—the first cantilevered chair made from a single piece of plastic. It was designed to look as if it were hovering in space. It was sexy and a technical breakthrough, and it became the chair of the era!

The lady that bought the desk organizer emailed me to say, "This neat piece has been sitting on the desk of my home office since I bought it. What is funny is that I imagined it to be much larger—so it is now a running joke with my husband. It has become friends with my Knoll Tulip desk chair and it has found a good home." Robyn

Too bad she doesn't have a Panton desk chair! By the way, my parents took my brother and I to Europe in the late 1960s and we also traveled the continent in a VW Bus. Crazy! I guess we were destined to become artists and writers. How cool is that?

# #53 Vasart Scottish Vase

$20.⁰⁰ Paid
From: Ad in the Antique Trader

**Stunning Vasart Art Glass Vase Scottish Vintage RARE**

**Description:**
Stunning art glass vase was hand made in Scotland and it still has the original paper label sticker. Very unusual to find a piece with this label still intact. 4¼" by 3¼". A hand blown beautiful piece in excellent condition. I would guess 1940s Eames era.

**Winning Bid:**

# $65.⁰⁰

**Ended:** 12/3/05
**History:** 8 bids
**Starting Bid:** $24.99
**Winner:** Glasgow, Scotland

**Viewed**
000089 X

# Vasart Scottish Vase #53

## The Story

Before eBay, if my grandmother had something expensive and wanted to sell it quickly, she had to place an advertisement in the *Antique Trader*. Oh, those were the days, my friend! We didn't even have digital cameras.

Back then, we would lay out the items and place identifying numbers by each one. Next we would take actual black and white pictures of the items, take the film to be developed, write a line of copy for each item, and assign each piece a price. Then we would send it all off to the *Antique Trader* in Dubuque, Iowa, and tell them we wanted to buy a small display ad for $100.

Finally, we would wait another two weeks for the ad to come out. After all that, we were lucky if we sold one piece. I'll tell you, mail-order for an antique business back in the 1960s to the 1990s was not easy. So, if any of you ever complain about how time-intensive eBay is—I will NOT listen.

In addition to advertising items for sale in the trader, my grandmother also ran a lot of "wanted to buy" ads over the years. Because I am always looking for new places to find merchandise, I placed a "wanted to buy" ad in the *Antique Trader*.

I spent about $25 and ran a four-line classified: "Wanted to buy China, Dinnerware, Antiques, RC, B&G, Collectibles, Flatware." The response was great, and I received five actual letters in the mail with photos and lists—just like my grandmother used to get in the 1960s to the 1990s! It was fun.

I bought this Vasart vase for $20 from one of the gentleman who responded to my *Antique Trader* ad. I also negotiated to buy two wonderful dinner sets from a former antiques dealer in northern California. It was so cool, because I did not have to leave my house to find merchandise!

Salvador Ysart (founder of Vasart) was born in Barcelona, Spain, in 1878 and moved to Scotland in 1914 to escape the war. He had four sons, and they all worked in the glass business.

The four boys and their father Salvador moved among different glass factories quite a bit—they worked for Moncrieff, Monart, Caithness, and Perthshire, to name a few. This family had a major influence on what we know as the Scottish paperweight factories of today.

In the mid-1940s, Salvador and two of his sons founded Vasart, and it remained in existence until 1965, when it was sold and renamed "Strathearn." Salvador died in 1955, and this vase is a wonderful example of the Ysarts' work.

I was very happy when it sold for $65 (tripling my money) and was shipped back to Scotland. Amazing! Doing business completely by mail order—just like my grandmother did even before there were computers! And way before eBay!

# #54 Heller G Coil Vase

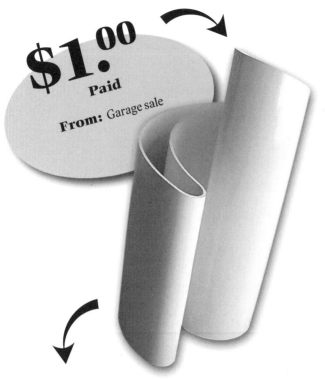

$1.⁰⁰ **Paid**

**From:** Garage sale

**Eames Heller Melmac Coil "G" Vase Giotto Stoppino RARE!**

### Description:

Rare vase is 1950s to 1960s Eames-era melmac melamine in a coil "G" letter shape. This is an amazing piece of retro mid-century modern design. A white/off white plastic for long stemmed flowers or to be used as a stand alone piece of art by Heller. Signed with "Giotto Stoppino," the designer and "Heller Italy." It goes from 8¼" at the lower twist to 14" tall. The base is 9" by 7". The coil is about 1½" wide with a thickness of ⅛". There are some very minor and faint scuffs and it needs cleaning. Otherwise in very good to excellent condition. These are very hard to find and rarely come up for sale.

**Winning Bid:**

# $51.⁵⁵

**Ended:** 12/3/05
**History:** 8 bids
**Starting Bid:** $9.99
**Winner:** Atlanta, GA

**Viewed**
**000122** X

# Heller G Coil Vase #54

## The Story

My mom and I were out garage saling and stumbled across a gigantic pile of army costumes, boots, and belts on the ground at one sale. My mom specializes in clothing, and that way we don't butt heads—at least not too often! I urged her to ask them how much for everything. She got a great deal and she is still selling those costumes—out of her eBay store!

At the same sale, I found this super neat vase (also sitting on the ground) for only a buck. My mom was heartbroken when she saw me buy it because it is from one of her favorite mid-century companies, Heller. I probably should have given it to her but I listed it on eBay instead.

It sold the day I was in Los Angeles for the USC vs. UCLA football game. Peter and I try to attend one a year, and this one was on his birthday weekend. We stayed at Shutters on the Beach in Santa Monica and had a really fun weekend. Shutters is such a cool hotel, and it was all decorated for Christmas. Besides, USC beat UCLA! Can't get better than that.

Peter used to work for Heller Financial in LA in the 1990s and this piece was made by Heller. Not the same company, however! This Heller Company was founded in 1971, and is an international furniture manufacturer with production in the US and Europe.

Oops! My date range for this piece was way off. Heller wasn't making any pieces in the real mid-century years of the Eames era, 1947 to 1969. They actually started right at the tail end of that time frame. Heller's first product was a line of stacking dinnerware designed by Massimo Vignelli. These dishes are pretty easy to find and I encourage you to pick them up when you see them because they sell great!

This G-coil vase that I sold was designed by Giotto Stoppino, who has managed his own studio of design in Milan since 1968. He specializes in architecture, interior decoration and design. His objects are exhibited in museums worldwide. He designed this piece for Heller sometime in the 1970s, and it is a combination of clever design coupled with advances in technology.

I was hoping that it would sell for close to $100—but it ended up selling for $51.55. For that, I should have kept it as a Christmas gift for my mom! Oops—oh, well. At 7:24 pm on Saturday, December 3rd, when it sold, Peter and I were having dinner at Chinois on Main—Wolfgang Puck's Santa Monica restaurant. That extra $50 sure came in handy to pay for Peter's birthday dinner—no free meals at that establishment!

# #55 Winnie-the-Pooh Ornament

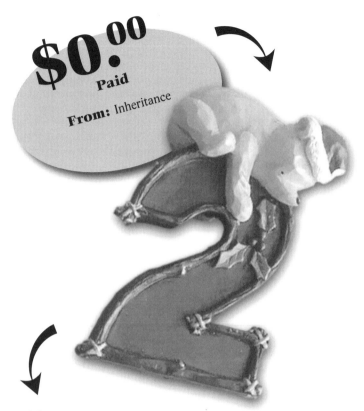

**$0.⁰⁰ Paid**

**From:** Inheritance

**Midwest Classic Pooh Disney 2 Two Christmas Ornament**

**Description:**
This darling ornament is about 2¾" by 1¾". Excellent condition and mint with the original tags. Never been used. From several years back. The number 2 has Winnie-the-Pooh hanging on the top. Use for Baby's Second Christmas or in the numbered series. So cute! We have a lot more Midwest of Cannon Falls and Dept. 56 items up for sale this week.

**Winning Bid:** **$49.⁸⁸**

**Ended:** 12/4/05
**History:** 14 bids
**Starting Bid:** $9.99
**Winner:** Orangeburg, SC

**Viewed**
000087 X

# Winnie-the-Pooh Ornament #55

## The Story

My home phone was ringing one day and I NEVER answered it back then because it was never for me. But my dad was visiting and he picked it up. Lucky thing! It turned out to be Nan Klein from Teletime Video in NY, and she was filming a segment for the USPS (United States Postal Service) about eBay sellers. Nan and I chatted a bit and we realized I was a great fit for their production. They wanted to feature me! How cool is that?

I ship about half by UPS and half by USPS. You half to (ha ha). UPS is awesome because they pick up at my house every day and their rates are very good. We love our UPS drivers. USPS is great, too, because they have super-quick service with Priority envelopes and boxes. AND we love all our postal counter employees in zip code 92255. So, we are big fans of both companies.

This little Winnie-the-Pooh ornament had been for sale in our antiques and gifts store in the Christmas room back in 1999, and its manufacturer's suggested retail (MSR) had been $9.95. I got it in one of the boxes that I had inherited from the shop. I thought I didn't have anything to lose, and put it on eBay with a starting bid of $9.99 and $5 shipping by USPS Priority!

But, back to the video production. We decided to do the filming in LA, since I would be there for the weekend with Peter, celebrating his birthday. The USPS crew would film me the Monday after he left. So I stayed an extra night at Shutters and met the film crew in the grass in front of the Santa Monica pier that next morning.

The shoot went very quickly and I think I did quite well. I have had a lot of experience being in front of a camera, so it was a fun day! I was just bummed that Peter couldn't stay for it, as he had to get back to work. You can still view this footage on the post office web site at www.usps.com.

When I finished the shoot, I went back to the hotel to pack up and head home. When I arrived back in Palm Desert at about 5 pm, I couldn't believe that the price on this piece was up to almost $50! Yikes. I was so glad that it hadn't sold in our store when we were closing and everything was 70% off—that would have brought in only $3.

I still can't figure out exactly why this ornament sold for so much, but I guess there are a lot of classic Winnie-the-Pooh collectors, and the number two made this piece a perfect gift for a baby's second birthday or Christmas. Someone in South Carolina wanted it pretty badly. Put Winnie-the-Pooh in a baby-themed Christmas ornament, retire it, and you have the recipe for a $50 success on eBay!

The buyer paid the same evening and the next day it was shipped out by USPS Priority—at the same time my video for the USPS was being edited back in NY.

USPS Promo Video

Lynn Dralle
eBay user ID: thequeenofauctions

# #56  Pam Schifferl Santa

$0.⁰⁰
**Paid**
**From:** Inheritance

## Midwest Pam Schifferl Christmas Ornament Retired Santa

**Description:**

This ornament is from the Folk Art Enchanted Winter's Eve collection designed by Pam Schifferl for Midwest. Has the tags and is in mint condition. Never displayed. 2¼" by 1¼". Cute! We have a lot of great Midwest of Cannon Falls and Dept. 56 Christmas items up for sale this month. All were items carried in our antiques and gifts store in the 1990s and are mostly retired pieces in mint condition with the original tags. They have been in storage for several years.

**Winning Bid:**

# $24.⁴⁵

**Ended:** 12/15/05
**History:** 6 bids
**Starting Bid:** $9.99
**Winner:** Washington, IN

**Viewed**
000036 X

# Pam Schifferl Santa  #56

## The Story

When my grandmother built her addition to the shop in 1976, she made her new apartment one huge room. She did this so that if someday the city would allow her to, she would make the new addition the shop and move back into the old house.

Well, in 1998, the shop was expanding like crazy (and by the way, so was my waistline—I was pregnant with Indiana). So my grandma and I decided that it was time to move part of the shop into her living space. We hired a contractor to wall off a portion of my grandmother's living room and put a door from the shop into the new section.

This new area was quite large—about 20' by 15'—and was going to become our Christmas room. We were so excited! We all love Christmas. So off we went to the Seattle Gift Show to do our ordering. For once, we could go nuts with Christmas ornaments and décor.

Audrey Mortensen (my original employee!) and I drove down and met Melanie (my best friend) at the Gift Show. Melanie has been in retail as long as I have and she is in management for Ikea. She has a great retail eye. We had appointments with Midwest of Cannon Falls, Yankee Candle, and Dept. 56, to name a few.

We three gals had a blast that day buying tons of new Christmas gift items for the new room. We spent about $20,000. I had never spent that much on Christmas before. Yikes!

When all the merchandise began to arrive in August, we had several of our fa-

mous evening work parties with music, wine, and all four of my employees. We worked hard to get that room looking great, and boy, did it ever!

When the shop closed in 2002, there was still quite a bit of Christmas stuff left over and it got divided up among my mom, brother, sister, and me. After the Winnie-the-Pooh ornament (story #55) sold for so much money, I headed out to my garage to look for more Christmas items. I was also eyeing all the Midwest ornaments on my own Christmas tree, but I slapped myself silly and refrained. I did find this Pam Schifferl ornament in the garage.

Midwest is one of my favorite Christmas companies. Located in Cannon Falls, Minnesota, it has sold to specialty retailers for more than 50 years (about as long as my grandma was in business). Their designs are artist-driven and created from scratch by their own in-studio team. One of those artists is Pam Schifferl, a third-generation carver whose charming designs are first hand-made and then mass-produced as Christmas décor.

Amazing that an ornament that has been retired for just a few years can sell for so much more than the original retail. This tiny Santa had an original retail price of only $5.95, so he cost us about $2.50 wholesale in 1998. Wow! Remember this if you are in retail stores that are selling obsolete and old merchandise—these items can turn into a pile of gold and be even better than new!

# #57  Big Griswold Skillet

$10.00 Paid
From: Estate sale

**15.5" RARE Huge Griswold Skillet 14 Cast Iron 718 Neat!**

### Description:

15½" huge Griswold skillet is very neat. Marked "14" and "718." I
have never seen one of these in this size. It is very large and hard
to find. It is in good to very good condition but has some scratches.
Some wear. Signed "Griswold Erie PA USA 718 A." It is flat and
does not rock. I just bought an incredible collection of antique and
vintage kitchen kitchenware items. I will be listing a lot of them in
the next few weeks.

**Winning Bid:**

# $153.50

**Ended:** 12/16/05
**History:** 6 bids
**Starting Bid:** $24.99
**Winner:** Plymouth, MI

**Viewed**
000322 X

# Big Griswold Skillet   #57

## The Story

Remember the day that my dad helped me pick up all that stuff, and my car bottomed out leaving the driveway? This was one of the items in that load, and after several months, I was finally getting around to listing it. The woman who had sold me the silverplated stuff had also collected kitchen items, and her garage cupboards were filled with them. I paid her $300 for it all—lock, stock, and barrel—and now my garage cupboards are filled with them.

Of course, you guessed it, my grandmother used to say "lock, stock and barrel" all the time. I knew that it meant the "whole thing," but I wanted to know how the phrase originated. One explanation claimed that it refers to all of a shopkeeper's stock in trade, the items stored in barrels, and the lock to the door. I have to admit this would have been my grandmother's favorite explanation, since she was the epitome of a shopkeeper!

But alas, it seems that when this phrase originated, it referred to the three parts of a musket: the lock (short for "flintlock"), that is the firing mechanism; the stock, which is the wooden butt end of the gun; and finally, the barrel, the cylindrical tubes through which the bullet travels. The earliest known use of this phrase is in letters from Sir Walter Scott in 1817. Apparently Scott wasn't shy about inventing new phrases in his writing.

Cast iron is a study in itself. Most cast iron cookware is produced in a sand mold made by packing special casting sand around a pattern. Because the sand mold has to be destroyed in order to remove the piece that has just been cast, each pan had to have its own mold. In order to create enough of these disposable sand molds, the company might need several patterns to produce the molds. A different letter (or no letter) would be used for each of the sand mold patterns for a specific style of pan. These letters then show up on the finished product.

Griswold cookware was made from 1865 to the late 1950s. Their first mark was just "Erie" because they were located in Erie, PA. The later Griswold trademark is a cross with two circles around it. The numbers on the back of each Griswold piece are important because they indicate the item's size. But, as far as collectors are concerned, there is nothing special about the letter on a pan; no letters are considered more or less valuable than the others. I didn't know that! I always thought I was going to find a RARE letter!

You can pick up Griswold pretty much everywhere. Only certain pieces will sell for big bucks, so don't overspend. It is very important to collectors that these pieces sit flat and do not rock. Condition is important.

Mo (my second assistant) used to yell at me to stop buying cast iron! I still have quite a few of the "lock, stock, and barrel" pieces parked in my eBay store. They will eventually sell for $9.99, but cast iron is a heavy and messy business. Oh, well, this one pan paid for half of my collection. "Yikes-Wow-Score!" I want to invent new phrases in my writing just like Sir Walter Scott did. What do you think of that one?

Yikes-Wow-Score!

# #58 Cherub Sterling Cordial

**$0.00 Paid**

**From:** Inheritance

**Comyns Antique Sterling Cherub Cordial Shot Glass NICE!**

### Description:

Comyns antique sterling shot glass is nice. This piece comes from my grandmother's personal collection and is so darling! Cherubs or angels working and playing in relief sterling. 2" by 1¼". There is an amber glass insert. Signed "WC" and 4 hallmarks. A rampant lion and what looks like a "T" and an "O" and a head. The lion passant/rampant means sterling and it is from England. I am guessing that the W.C. is for William Comyns & Sons, 1885 to 1953. I would date this piece to the 1890s to early 1900s. A darling piece that needs polishing. I will let the new owner do that. In great condition.

**Winning Bid:** **$33.00**

**Ended:** 12/16/05
**History:** 14 bids
**Starting Bid:** $9.99
**Winner:** Palm Coast, FL

**Viewed**
000043 X

# Cherub Sterling Cordial   #58

## The Story

My grandmother loved anything with cherubs or angels on it, so she collected those items. I think her love of cherubs began when she was a little girl. After her mother died, everyone would tell her that she was such a sweet baby and it was so sad that her mother had left her because she looked just like a cherub.

I have always wondered what the difference between a cherub and an angel is—so I decided to find out. By the way, I always put both in my title if there is room. A cherub is defined as a sweet innocent baby (my grandmother) or an angelic creature whose distinctive attribute is knowledge (also my grandmother) and is usually portrayed as a winged child. Cherubim (the plural of "cherub") are usually thought of as guardians.

An angel is defined as a spiritual being acting as a messenger of God, and is usually depicted as a human-type creature with wings. Angels, including cherubs, protect and guide us.

I have now decided that this is definitely a cherub piece because the angels were childlike. It was signed with "WC" and the English hallmark (rampant lion) for sterling. I found that "WC" stood for William Comyns & Sons.

William Comyns completed his apprenticeship at the Goldsmiths' Hall in London in 1856 at age 22. He was given the freedom to work anywhere in the city of London and a gold charm for good work and conduct. He eventually began his own business (William Comyns) in 1859 in the west end of London.

In 1885 he went into business with his two sons, Charles and Richard. The company was then known as William Comyns and Sons. With the addition of the younger generation, the company had enormous success in the 1880s and produced a vast amount of goods that were retailed to the public. They sold to many of the top shops of the day, including Tiffany & Co. Their specialty was Victorian and Edwardian designs. William passed away in 1913, but the business survived until 1953.

One of my grandmother's favorite museums in the world was the Victoria and Albert Museum in London. I found it especially interesting that the museum today has the working papers of many early artists and silversmiths. In fact, the Victoria and Albert museum has extensive records from the William Comyns and Sons Ltd., who held over thirty thousand silverware patterns and created all the coronets for the queens' coronations. Cool!

I don't think my grandmother knew all this history when she decided to keep this precious cherub piece in her collection. This piece ended up selling for $33, and I believe that someone is always watching over me. I am sure that my grandmother is my guardian angel.

# #59 Wham-O Magic Window

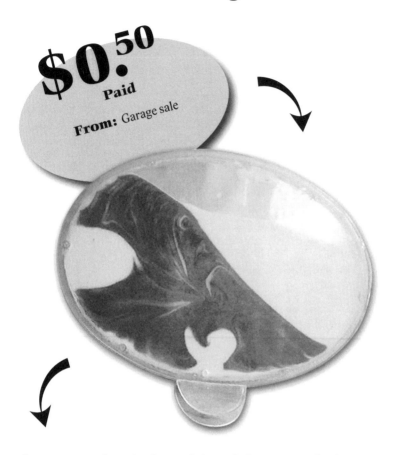

$0.<sup>50</sup> Paid

From: Garage sale

**Wham-O Magic Window with Original Stand Vintage COOL!**

### Description:
Wham-O Magic window with original stand. Vintage and very cool. 10¼" by 7". The sand moves well through this piece—sticks a little bit around the edges. Minor scratches. In overall very good condition. Comes with the hard-to-find original stand.

**Winning Bid:**

# $56.<sup>55</sup>

**Ended:** 12/16/05
**History:** 18 bids
**Starting Bid:** $9.99
**Winner:** Rensselaer, IN

**Viewed**
000102 X

# Wham-O Magic Window  #59

## The Story

I was at a tacky garage sale. Could there even be such a thing? Yes, of course. You know what I am talking about. Clothes strewn on the ground, everything looks like it should have been thrown away years ago, and to top it all off, everything is filthy.

I was doing my usual quick walk-in and walk-out when I spotted this Magic Window on the table. "Wow!" I said to my mom, "I remember these from when I was a kid." Ding! Ding! Ding!—that little bell went off in my head and I decided to buy it because it was only 50 cents, and sometimes I do take my own advice. (Remember, if it reminds you of being a kid—buy it).

It also had a tiny piece of plastic that acted as a stand. Interestingly enough, I don't remember having a stand for mine. Most of the stands got lost or thrown away, and that is why the ones with the stands sell for the most money.

The Wham-o company was started by two friends (Richard Knerr and Arthur "Spud" Melin) in a Los Angeles, CA garage in 1948. Aren't the best businesses started in garages? I think I could say that is where my eBay business started! What about yours?

In 1957, the still-struggling company came up with the idea of marketing an Australian bamboo exercise hoop to America. The name "hula hoop" had been used since the eighteenth century. The hula hoop turned into one of the biggest fads of all times. In four months, the company had sold 25 million!

Wham-O's next big hit came when Knerr and Merlin bought the rights to a flying disc called the "Pluto platter" from a man named Fred Morrison. They modified the design and re-named it (you guessed it) the Frisbee. It was launched in 1959.

In 1973, they came out with the Magic Window in two styles: a combination of white, black and blue, and a glow-in-the-dark version in white, hot pink and yellow.

Contrary to popular belief, the Magic Window does not contain "sand". The contents are tiny glass beads of various colors and sizes that give the window its magic! These toys were put together in a "clean room" setting.

Wham-O is also responsible for silly string and the slip-n-slide. Houston currently owns a slip-n-slide and Indiana has several hula hoops. Timeless! And what a cool company! It is amazing how fast a favorite toy can transport us back in time. Thanks for the memories, Wham-O! And the $56!

# #60  Precious Moments Nativity

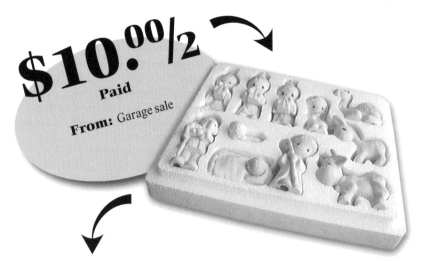

$10.⁰⁰/2
Paid
**From:** Garage sale

**Precious Moments Mini MIB Nativity Accessories E 2387**
**Precious Moments Mini MIB 11 pc Nativity Set RARE 2395**

### Description:

This Nativity Accessories E 2387 is rare and hard to find. The box is 9.5" by 6.5" by 3.5". Bisque set from 1982. Three buildings and a palm tree. Great set and mint in box—still in the plastic. Looks like it has never been displayed. It is not too late for Christmas delivery.

This eleven piece nativity set 2395 is rare and hard to find. From 1982! Box is 10" by 8¼" by 3". Looks like it has never been displayed and it is not to late for Christmas delivery. Made from bisque.

The history of Precious Moment's Sugar Town: "When Precious Moments artist Sam Butcher created Sugar Town, it was to honor the people, places and events that have shaped his life. Every building, every person portrayed have touched Sam's life in a very special way and he wants to share it with you. It's an irresistible vignette of family life portraying one of the most beautiful and cherished moments as only Sam Butcher can express it...in a spirit of loving, caring and sharing... Welcome to Sugar Town...Sam's special gift to you."

**Winning Bid:** $226.⁴⁹/2

**Ended:** 12/17/05
**History:** 33 bids/2
**Starting Bid:** $9.99 each
**Winner:** NY and GA

**Viewed**
 X

# Precious Moments Nativity #60

## The Story

It was December 10th and I had not figured out what we were going to do for a Christmas card. This is so not like how I used to be, but my life has become really hectic! Time goes by so quickly. Remember when you were a kid and it seemed like an eternity until Christmas arrived? Well, now it seems like Christmas comes right after Easter!

So, while I was worrying about the fact that I hadn't scheduled a photo shoot for the card and that it was too late to finish the cards before Christmas, my mom and I hit a really great garage sale. On the ground in a big plastic tub was a huge collection of Precious Moments. The man wanted $300 for the whole set, and while I knew nothing about these figurines, I had a hunch.

There were over 60 pieces, all still mint in box—so on average they cost me $5 each. I put these two nativity sets on eBay the day I found them (well, actually that evening) because I wanted bidders to be able to get them in time for Christmas. I guess I care more about my customers than my friends and family, because they certainly weren't going to get Christmas cards from me in time for the holidays!

Sam Butcher was born in 1939 in Jackson, Michigan. His family was very poor and as a child he remembers his grandmother telling him Bible stories. He painted scenes from the stories he heard, sometimes on rocks because his family could not afford paper. This lead to a career as a "chalk board minister," using illustrations to teach young children about God.

In 1974, Sam started an inspirational greeting card business which featured his teardrop-eyed children. He called them "Precious Moments" because he hoped they would spread love, caring, and sharing in everyday situations.

In 1978, the Enesco Company transformed Sam's artwork into bisque figurines. The original 21 pieces were produced that year. Imagine what they sell for if mine from four years later went so high.

While overseas on business, Sam lost his 27-year-old son Phillip in an auto accident. Sam remembers him as one of the funniest and cutest kids ever, with a very loving heart. His favorite song was "It's a Wonderful World."

Sam had a hard time dealing with his grief until he began painting Phillip's room in a chapel that he had built at the foot of the Missouri Ozarks. The chapel features a mural of Phillip being welcomed into heaven, his family below him. Sam was able to remember in paint a son whose unexpected death had left a painful emptiness within his heart.

It is no wonder that these two early pieces of Enesco both sold for over $100 each. While I was working on this auction, I remembered an amazing photo that my brother had taken at the beach by his house earlier that year. It would be perfect for our Christmas card. The inside said, "Celebrate and God Bless." Every time I look at this picture I am reminded that these are my Precious Moments and that I need to slow down and enjoy them.

# #61 Dept 56 Mission Church

$10.<sup></sup>**00**

Paid

**From:** Garage sale

**Vintage RARE Dept 56 Snowhouse 1980 Mission Church HTF**

**Description:**
Vintage early Dept. 56 is signed on the base with "Mission Church ©
Dept. 56" and a sticker that says "Original 1980 Snowhouse Snow
house made in Taiwan." It does have the light and cord. 9" by 9½" by
5¼". There is a tiny chip on the tree. Four of the wood beams coming
out of the church have dings/nicks. Otherwise in great condition for
being over 25 years old. Very rare and hard to find piece.

**Winning Bid:** $595.<sup></sup>**43**

**Ended:** 12/18/05
**History:** 15 bids
**Starting Bid:** $9.99
**Winner:** Cannon Falls, MN

**Viewed**
000488 X

# Dept 56 Mission Church #61

## The Story

My mom and I were at a garage sale in a more industrial part of town, and the people had a ton of stuff. There were toys mint in the package and a lot of Christmas items. The prices were way too high, so I asked for a deal on some of the Christmas items. The lady said, "No way." The sale had just started and she was going to "tough it out" as my grandmother would have said.

It turned out that all the toys belonged to her son, so I thought I would try my luck with him. I asked for a deal on a huge box full of mint-in-package Star Wars action figures. He was more reasonable and offered them to me at $3 each, so I bought them. I was still drawn to the Christmas items, but they were priced way too high, so we left.

After driving to six other sales, I suggested to my mom that we go back and see if the lady was ready to *negotiate*. My grandmother was a stickler about "dickering" (her term for bargaining) in the antique store. It wasn't allowed. Her prices were firm and I respected her for that. She had a really funny sign that hung in the shop stating this to her customers.

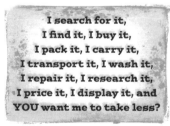

I search for it,
I find it, I buy it,
I pack it, I carry it,
I transport it, I wash it,
I repair it, I research it,
I price it, I display it, and
YOU want me to take less?

So, we arrived back at the sale and I picked up the two ceramic Christmas villages that were on the ground. One was marked $45 and the other $25. You have got to be kidding to price that high at a garage sale.

Reality had set in and I asked the lady for a better price. She looked at them and said, "How about $20 for both?" Now that was more like it. In retrospect, I could have paid the $70 and still have come out smelling like a rose!

It turned out that the Mission Church was signed "Dept. 56." In 1976, a premier florist in Minneapolis called Bachman's developed a numbering system to identify each of its departments. The number assigned to the gift imports division was...drum roll please...Dept. 56.

That is so funny because when I was an executive trainee at May Department stores, I was the assistant buyer for Dept. 74, kitchen appliances, and then my first buying position was for Dept. 73, vacuums. Seriously, not as exciting as gift imports!

Dept. 56 is still in business and is a very successful collectibles company located in Eden Prairie, MN. Funny that both Midwest of Cannon Falls and Dept. 56 are in Minnesota. In 1976, Dept. 56 introduced six charming, lighted ceramic buildings. They were the foundation of the company.

In December of 1979, the Mission Church was added to the Dept. 56 line and it was retired exactly one year later, in December of 1980. This was one rare church that I had stumbled across. It ended up selling for $595.43 in December of 2005—exactly 25 years after it had been retired—and was shipped to Cannon Falls, MN (home of rival Midwest). Strange!

As another strange ending note, the church arrived in pieces—broken, shattered. What a tragedy. I hate it when anything arrives broken, especially such a rare piece. Luckily, we

# #62 Pince Nez Glasses

$0.$^{00}$ Paid
From: Inheritance

**Pince Nez Nose Pinch Antique Eyeglass Glasses Fits You**

### Description:
Pince Nez Nose Pinch eyeglasses. "Fits You" is the brand name with an "A" in a circle. 4" by 1¼". In very good condition. Some patina. A hole in the right hand side for a chain. 1900s or so. The case is in as-is condition.

**Winning Bid:**

# $34.$^{65}$

**Ended:** 12/19/05
**History:** 6 bids
**Starting Bid:** $9.99
**Winner:** Minot, ND

**Viewed**

000032 X

# Pince Nez Glasses  #62

## The Story

In 1993, when we started redoing the shop and going through back cupboards, I would often come across entire shoe boxes of items that were sorted but not priced.

My grandmother had a ton of stuff, but she knew exactly where everything was stored. If you needed to find antique eyeglasses, she would say, "Go into the back bedroom and on about the middle shelf on the left-hand side you will find a shoe box marked 'eye glasses.'"

Bull's eye! She was never wrong. We had a huge shoebox full of antique glasses and no way to price them. (Remember, there was no Priceminer and no eBay back in 1993). So my grandmother suggested we get in touch with one of the people who used to help in the shop, John Handley, who was now the manager of the medical history collection at the American Academy of Ophthalmology in San Francisco. We couldn't have asked for a better expert!

My grandmother had hired a lot of part-time help over the years and basically she was just too trustworthy. Quite a few of these so called "helpers" ended up stealing from her. In fact, when we were all in Italy for my spring break in 1984, she got a phone call from my dad saying that the lady watching the shop had been picked up at the Canadian border with a car full of merchandise stolen from Cheryl Leaf Antiques. It was always a huge risk that, with so much stock, some unscrupulous types would decide to help themselves.

But this was never the case with John Handley—in fact, he is the nicest and most trustworthy guy you can imagine. My grandmother always thought the world of John, so she wrote him a letter to see if we could pay him for some help on the eye glasses. "No problem," he wrote back.

I took photos of the glasses and sent them off to John. He wrote back saying he thought they were worth about $25. Well, they never sold in the shop for that price, so I inherited them and decided to try them on eBay.

They were pince-nez, a style of spectacles very popular in the 19th century. The name comes from the French for "pinch nose" because they are held on to the face by a spring that grips the nose. I tell you, I hate wearing eyeglasses because they irritate my ears—this could be my answer.

Pince-nez were often hung from a ribbon or chain worn around the neck, or attached to a hairpin.

Teddy Roosevelt wore pince-nez glasses, and they were once again in the spotlight when Lawrence F burne's character, Morpheus, wc them in the Matrix trilogy in the late 1990s. Cool!

Maybe that is why they sold for $34.65, way more than they would have sold for in my grandmother's antiques store.

I just got a note from John and he writes, "I have such great memories of your grandmother and think about her still. She taught me a lot and was also a great friend." Thank you for sharing, John—I feel the exact same way about her.

# #63 Radko Train Ornament

**$3.**<sup>33</sup>

**From:** Garage sale

## Christopher Radko Toy Train Express Santa Ornament MIB

### Description:
This darling toy train ornament by Radko comes mint in the original box. Santa Claus head or face is the front of the train and a number #25 is painted on the side. 4.5" by 2" by 4" with the original tags. Vintage and in excellent condition. I would guess that this piece is retired and hard to find.

**Winning Bid:**

**$112.**<sup>50</sup>

**Ended:** 12/19/05
**History:** 20 bids
**Starting Bid:** $9.99
**Winner:** Douglasville, GA

**Viewed**

000155 X

# Radko Train Ornament  #63

## The Story

If you think that my son Houston's first love was baseball, you would be wrong. His first love was choo-choo trains. From before he could walk, he was fascinated with trains. For his third birthday, he got the entire Thomas the Tank collection, with the train table and the huge train toy box. This was back when I was making a lot of money with the Beanie Baby books. Those were the good ol' days!

After he grew tired of Thomas, it was on to Lionel cast iron steam engines with real smoke. I spent a fortune on trains over the years. When Ty (the maker of Beanie Babies) sued my brother and me and we had to pay them a settlement, destroy our books and so on, it ruined our company, AKA publishing. The A was for my middle initial, the K for my sister's middle initial and the final A for my brother's middle initial. We thought it was rather clever.

But in the course of ten days, I had to come up with a new name for my publishing company, which had moved from Beanie Babies on to eBay-related products. My grandmother's advice about naming a business was to use the first letters in the alphabet because then you would be listed first in the phone book.

Great advice for when people actually used phone books—but I do think that it still has some value.

As I was struggling to find a business name, my brother came up with "All Aboard, Inc." in honor of Houston's love of trains. Cute! My grandmother approved of all the A's, and we were once again in business.

Whenever I see trains at garage sales, I usually pick them up. Old habits die hard. I found this darling Radko Christmas ornament at a sale and it was bundled with two other Christmas ornaments for $10. I tried to get the gentleman to take less, but he was the same guy who sold me all the Precious Moments figurines and he wouldn't budge. I forked over a $10 bill.

Christopher Radko's company began in 1984 because of a tragedy. Radko's family Christmas tree was decorated with 2,000 mouth-blown European glass ornaments. The Christmas tree stand gave way and caused the tree to crash to the floor, breaking most of the ornaments. Along with the ornaments went years of memories and stories.

Fast forward to today: because of Radko's perseverance in recovering antique molds, working in Europe with glass blowers, and designing new ornaments, the company has created over 10,000 different ornament designs. Radko ornaments can be found in the White House, in orphanages and in many celebrity homes.

The Radko company's motto is that a Christopher Radko ornament is more than just an ornament—it is a "work of heart!" It's funny, but we just created a motto for my website, and it is "eBay with heart!" It's no wonder that this darling train ornament sold for over $100!

# #64  Erzgebirge Carousel Pyramid

$12.<sup>50</sup>

**Paid**

**From:** Charity sale

## BIG Christmas Erzgebirge Carousel Pyramid Windmill RARE

### Description:

Huge vintage carousel pyramid windmill is rare. This wonderful piece is signed "Original Erzgebirge Made in German Democratic Republic Expertic." I would guess 1950s to 1970s and vintage. About 24" tall and 10" wide. In Scandinavia these are called "angel bells." Some wear and missing pieces. Manger nativity scene with Mary Joseph and Baby Jesus. Quite a few farm animals and the three wise men.

**Winning Bid:**

$86.<sup>61</sup>

**Ended:** 12/22/05
**History:** 18 bids
**Starting Bid:** $9.99
**Winner:** Scottsdale, AZ

**Viewed**
000104 X

# Erzgebirge Carousel Pyramid  #64

## The Story

I had bought this neat Christmas piece back in October, but it was like a white elephant in my eBay room. You know those items that are big and complicated and you just keep procrastinating and they never seem to make it on eBay.

Well, I bit the bullet (another Cheryl Leaf favorite saying) in December and finally got it listed. I figured Christmas was the perfect time to sell it. "Biting the bullet" means "enduring pain with strength"; the phrase has it roots on the battleground. Before anesthetics, soldiers were given bullets to bite on to help them endure the pain of surgery.

This carousel had been marked $25 at a charity sale, but I was there on the last day and picked it up for $12.50. It reminded me of a Scandinavian Christmas piece, and I wasn't too far off.

This was signed "Erzgebirge" and came from Germany. The Erzgebirge is a mountainous region between Germany and the Czech border; it is also known as the Ore Mountains. The Ergzebirge has been covered in large forests since the pre-medieval times. In the fifteenth century, mining was the only industry. "Erz" means metal ore, and "gebirge" means mountain range. By the nineteenth century, the area's ore deposits were depleted and the people who lived in the Erzgebirge needed to make a living from something else, so they turned to their last remaining natural resource—the forests. It was then that they began to earn a living from wood crafting—particularly toys and collectibles.

Light is a central theme in a lot of Erzgebirge folk art, in part because of the Erzgebirge inhabitants' long history of mining in dark caverns underground, where they were dependent upon artificial illumination. Even though the last mine was closed in 1849, Erzgebirgen folk art still features light as a theme, and much of it actually uses candle light.

Christmas candle pyramids are a popular type of folk art, and a perfect fit for the artisans of the Erzgebirge, with their interest in light. Candle pyramids are made of a diorama on a carousel which turns when the candles' heat rises to meet the angled blades. The tiers on the carousal generally show biblical scenes or pictures of the rural or mining life.

About the time my candle pyramid was selling, I was featured in a half-page article in Country Home Magazine's Christmas edition. It is a really slick magazine from the Meredith Corporation and has a circulation of 1.25 million! They did a really nice job and used a photo that my brother had taken of me. My brother, given photography credit in a major national magazine. Too cool!

This German piece from the Erzgebirge region turned out to be a very profitable white elephant—and sold for over $80! Just as the people from the Ore Mountains had to use their natural resources to make a living, so has my family. My brother uses his artistic talent and the control of light to take amazing pictures, and I use my grandmother's instincts to smoke out bargains!

# #65 Demitasse Spoon Holder

$1.00
Paid
From: Garage sale

**Holland Dutch Antique Sterling Silver Spoon Holder RARE
Demitasse Spoon Rack Frame Floral Art Nouveau Hallmarks**

**Description:**
Holland Dutch sterling silver spoon holder is an amazing piece. It is a spoon rack holder or frame for a smaller spoon—such as a demitasse spoon. It is 6.5" by 5.25". Auction does not come with any spoons. It is signed or stamped on the top level with "Holland," "90" and some hallmarks. I can not make them out. I believe that "90" is the Dutch mark for sterling. This piece is very beautiful and ornate. Very art nouveau. I would date it from 1900s to 1950s. It has captured my attention and curiosity. Needs slight polish—in great condition.

**Winning Bid:** **$56.00**

**Ended:** 12/22/05
**History:** 2 bids
**Starting Bid:** $49.99
**Winner:** Portland, OR

**Viewed**
000088 X

# Demitasse Spoon Holder #65

## The Story

In the summer of 2005, the cutoff dates for baseball players' birthdays were rolled back for my son's league. This was wonderful news for us, because Houston was playing on a team with players who were almost a year older than he was. His birthday is in July and the cutoff was August 1st, so he was always the youngest kid on the team. Definitely not an advantage.

The new cutoff would allow Houston to play with younger kids, and as a consequence he was heavily recruited by nine-year-old teams. Yes, in Southern California, they do recruit nine-year-olds (this probably happens all over the U.S.—baseball is the national pastime, after all). One of Houston's best buddies, Brett, played for a team of nine-year-olds coached by his dad, Mike Ghelber, and Chris Bash. We were thrilled to join the team.

Houston started practicing in September with his new team, the Aztecs. One of our first tournaments was in December (while this piece was selling) in Chula Vista. We were a pretty green team and no one expected us to do well.

It was thrilling because we got to play against a team that Trevor Hoffman's sons played on. Hoffman is a closing pitcher for the San Diego Padres. It was a roller coaster of a tournament, but lo and behold, our Aztecs made it to the finals.

In the last inning of the championship game, they brought my son in to pitch. I was standing by the announcers when they said, "Here is Houston Wilson to pitch the final inning." The guys watching the game next to me were talking to one another, saying, "He is their closer." I said, "That's my son!" and I was so proud.

Houston shut down the Longhorns (9 to 8) and we won our first tournament with his new team. We were all so excited we were jumping up and down!

It's funny, but this really neat sterling spoon holder was so beautiful that for once, I didn't think the title alone could do it justice, so I added a sub-title to help it sell better. I rarely use a sub-title because it doubles all the listing fees. I started this piece at $49.99 because I couldn't find anything about it in my research and I didn't want to give it away at $9.99 the first time at auction.

The word that was important in the sub-title was "demitasse." "Demitasse" is a French word that means "half cup." This half cup holds about three ounces and is typically used for serving espresso. The spoons that you use with a demitasse cup are also smaller.

The sub-title seemed to help, because my $1 investment sold for $56 on the Thursday after the Aztecs won the Chula Vista tournament.

Now, whenever the boys are having a tough time in a tournament, we scream "Chula Vista!" to remind them of that incredible win! By the way, my son Houston now has a sub-title as well—it is "The Closer." And the Padres' closer, Trevor Hoffman, was very nice to my half-size closer, Houston. He posed for pictures, signed baseballs and even commented on how well Houston pitched!

# #66  Pair Alabaster Lamps

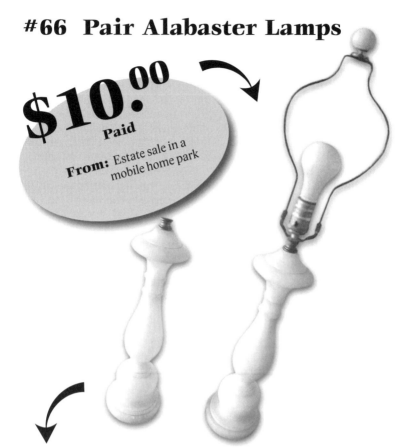

$10.00 Paid

From: Estate sale in a mobile home park

**Alabaster Marble Vintage PAIR Table Lamps Eames Era Wht**

**Description:**
This is a lovely set of matched table lamps. 30" to the top of the alabaster matching round finials. 17" to the top of the alabaster. I would guess 1930s to 1950s classic Eames era. They are in very good to excellent condition. Just need the perfect shades. The wiring looks to be in good condition, but you may want to rewire them just to be safe. These are very hard to find in a matched pair. Some very slight wear and they need cleaning. Very heavy. Super set.

**Winning Bid:** $381.00

**Ended:** 1/17/06
**History:** 31 bids
**Starting Bid:** $9.99, $150 reserve
**Winner:** New York, NY

**Viewed**
000436 X

# Pair Alabaster Lamps   #66

## The Story

It was a Friday in January and there were not many garage sales listed for that weekend. My mom called me early and said, "There is an estate sale in a trailer park that sounds pretty good." I don't usually find things in trailer parks but it sounded promising. It is ironic because my grandmother's brother, Houston, owned and lived in a trailer park in Calipatria, CA.

We walked in and whoever lived there was a collector. Knickknacks were all over—perfume bottles, cranberry glass and a ton of small items. I started asking, "How much?" and they man kept saying, "That is sold, that is sold." Then two dealers walked out of the bedroom. Yikes! We were fifteen minutes too late.

I don't mind missing things if I don't know that I missed them. Does that make sense? When I know that I missed them—it kills me!

So I asked if there was anything left in the bedroom that the two ladies had not purchased and they told me about a pair of white lamps that they would be happy to let me buy. I dejectedly walked in to take a look. They were only $10 and they were alabaster white marble. Score!

You may remember that I also wrote about a pair of alabaster lamps in *Money Making Madness* (story #37) but couldn't resist adding these to my new book because they sold for sooo much more and ended up in such an unusual place!

Alabaster is a type of marble that is usually white or grey with streaks. It was used a lot in the 1950s for lamps and sculptures. I think these lamps were unusual because they were almost all white and in excellent condition. Matched pairs sell the best.

I put them on eBay with a $9.99 starting price and a reserve of $150. I rarely use reserves, but thought that these lamps were worth at least $150 and I would wait it out for the right bidder. I didn't have to wait long, and these sold on a Tuesday afternoon in January for almost $400! Amazing!

What was even more amazing was the email I got from the buyer:

> Hi Lynn – I'm happy for you to include the lamps in the book. I'm sorry to say that they're with my ex! I bought them for our country house in East Hampton, NY, and to the best of my knowledge, that's where they still reside. Good luck with the book. -Keith

East Hampton is a village on the easternmost point of the south shore of Long Island and is surrounded by water on three sides. It has a reputation as a "playground of the rich" for anybody with major money.

The median price of a home in East Hampton in April of 2007 was $1,295,000. Celebrities with homes in the area include Jerry Seinfeld, Martha Stewart, and Kim Basinger.

What a story—from a trailer park in California to a "tony" house in East Hampton, NY. These lamps now live in the lap of luxury. Something else my grandmother would have said!

# #67 Butterick 1928 Catalog

**$0.00** Paid

**From:** Inheritance

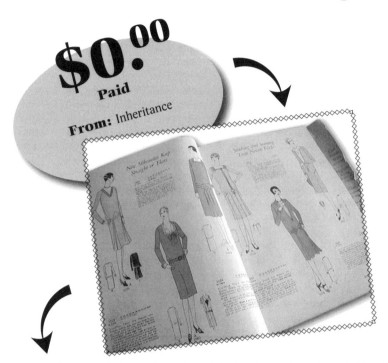

**Butterick Fashions Catalog 1928 Huge Roaring 20's NEAT**

### Description:

Butterick Fashions catalog is from February 1928. This is the neatest catalog. Says "Complete including transfer needle art." It is 12" by 14" and has a ton of pages. In OK condition. The price was $2.00 or $2.25 by mail Butterick Paris NY London. Someone started using this as a scrap book, so in the first few 10 or so pages there are glued pieces of scrap—some even Halloween. There is writing on some pages and there are some cut outs. Still it is a really neat piece of history that shows roaring '20s and styles that were in favor right before the great Depression. It goes up to page 555. A really neat piece of history.

**Winning Bid:**

**$79.59**

**Ended:** 1/24/06
**History:** 6 bids
**Starting Bid:** $24.99
**Winner:** Coupeville, WA

**Viewed**
**000130** X

## The Story

When my parents built our home in Bellingham on Bayside Road in the Edgemoor neighborhood in 1974, my mom and dad designed it. It was an awesome house overlooking the San Juan Islands. I lived in it from 7th grade until 12th grade and then every summer during college. My dad sold the house in 1990, and I cried about it for a month. Strange how you can get so attached to a home. It still makes me sad when I drive by it.

My mom is an amazing seamstress and designer. She owned a boutique in the Fairhaven section of Bellingham from 1974 until 1978 and in our new Edgemoor house she had a sewing room with a fabric room attached. Sounds like someone else I talk about a lot–possibly her mother, Cheryl Leaf. You can never have enough storage rooms with floor-to-ceiling shelves.

This room amazed me as a kid. It was filled with bolts and bolts of fabric. I was dragged around from a tender age to every fabric store from Portland, OR, to Bellingham, WA. I hated it. No wonder I never wanted to cook or sew.

But my mom loved it and she was very, very talented. Actually, she still is, and I am trying to talk her into becoming a designer. I think she and Indiana could start a granddaughter/grandmother design company. It is never too late to follow your passion.

So, when I found this old Butterick pattern book in with the stuff that I had inherited, I just knew that it would sell on eBay.

Butterick's history is amazing and rich. In 1863 in Sterling, Massachusetts, Ellen Butterick brought out her sewing basket to make a dress for her baby.

She used chalk to draw the design, and remarked to her husband, Ebenezer (a tailor), how much easier it would be if she had a pattern to refer to that was just the size of her son (yes, boys wore dresses in the 1860s).

There were patterns then, but the sewers had to either enlarge or reduce them. After much experimentation, Ebenezer created the first graded sewing patterns made from tissue paper.

Butterick's invention changed the fashion world forever. Before the graded pattern, fashion was exclusive to the rich and famous. No one could afford to pay for the latest styles from Paris until these patterns made dressmaking easy and affordable!

In 1867, Butterick published its first magazine with many more publications to follow. My Butterick pattern book was published in 1928, right before the great Depression. Butterick survived these years because when money is tight, people turn to handcrafts. Butterick is a thriving company today with home sewing patterns still the backbone of the company.

I think that there is time for my mother (with Indy's help) to also change the fashion world forever with her designs. She just needs to follow her passion! And get back to making those crazy patchwork creations she was famous for in the 1970s. Then we can pool our money (I've got almost $80 from this sale) and buy back our Edgemoor home (always my mom's dream).

# #68 Winnie-the-Pooh Bookends

**$8.00** Paid

**From:** Thrift store

### RARE Classic Winnie-the-Pooh Bookends Charpente Darling

**Description:**

Classic bookends are darling. This is an awesome pair of book ends. Disney Pooh and friends by Charpente Michel & Co. They don't have the sticker on the base but I have seen these marked with Charpente and this style rarely comes up for sale. Muted colors are so great in a nursery. Christopher Robin is putting on his boots on one side and Pooh is eating honey on the other end. They are made to appear to be carved out of wood, but I believe that they are heavy resin. High quality and in excellent condition. Measure 9¼" by 6¼" by 4" when pushed together.

**Winning Bid:**

**$43.02**

**Ended:** 1/24/06
**History:** 13 bids
**Starting Bid:** $9.99
**Winner:** Phillipsburg, NJ

**Viewed**
**000072 X**

# Winnie-the-Pooh Bookends #68

## The Story

When Indy was born, her daddy started a Winnie-the-Pooh Beanie Baby collection for her. Those Beanie Babies still look so cute on a shelf in her room (even though her room is now pink and princess in theme). She has every single one, from Engineer Winnie to Mother's Day Winnie and even Hannukah Winnie. Every time her dad traveled, he would bring one home for her. She was such a sweet baby and is still an amazing young lady.

I know that Disney sells well on eBay, but I didn't know just how well Pooh sells until I picked up these bookends for $8 at my thrift store. I figured that even if I couldn't get my $8 back, they would look darling in Indy's room.

Winnie-the-Pooh's history is quite complex and started way before Walt Disney ever got ahold of the licensing. Now, if I could just get Disney to license me—I would be set for life!

We have all heard about "Winnie-the-Pooh" bear, often referred to as "Pooh," who was created by A.A. Milne. The Pooh books were written in 1926 and 1928, and Pooh also appeared in some poems. All of the writings about Pooh were illustrated by E.H. Shepard.

Pooh was a toy bear owned by the author's son, Christopher Robin Milne. His official birthdate is August 21, 1921, the day of Christopher's first birthday, when he received him as a gift.

A.A. Milne and his son, Christopher, never made much money from the Winnie-the-Pooh franchise. In the 1930s, Milne sold the merchandise, television, and other U.S. and Canadian trade rights to Stephen Slesinger, a New York literary agent and producer. Stephen is also known as a pioneer in the licensing of characters for children.

Slesinger is responsible for changing Shepard's original drawings into the well known Americanized version that wears the red shirt. Keep in mind that there is classic Pooh, based on those older drawings, as well as the newer Pooh.

Slesinger died in the 1950s, and his widow Shirley took over the company. It was Slesinger Inc. that licensed some of the exclusive rights to the Walt Disney Company in 1961, and then again in 1983. Clare Milne (Christopher Robin's daughter) attempted to terminate any future US copyrights for Stephen Slesinger, Inc., but the US Court of Appeals granted in favor of Slesinger, Inc. in 2006. Disney also tried to terminate the licensing agreements with Slesinger Inc., but in 2007 the courts once again ruled in Slesinger's favor. Poor Winnie-the-Pooh—being dragged in and out of court.

I think my bookends sold for over $40 because they were the classic Pooh, which I think probably sells for more than the newer red-shirted Pooh.

What is really important to remember when looking at Disney items to sell on eBay, is that it is estimated that Winnie-the-Pooh merchandise generate as much revenue as Mickey Mouse, Minnie Mouse, Donald Duck, Goofy and Pluto combined. Pooh brings Disney from two to six billion dollars a year. Grab the Pooh items first!

# #69  Oak Children's Chair

$5.00
**Paid**
**From:** Garage sale

## Oak Children's Childs Baby Antique Chair Spindles CUTE!

### Description:

This is a darling oak chair. 7 spindles in the curved back. I would guess 1920s to 1930s Mission era oak. In very good to excellent condition. There are two splits in the curved wood—one at the top and one on the side. Also the front seat looks a little catawampus (crooked) from here. It was painted at some point in its past—as almost all good oak pieces were! You can see some of the different colors if you look at the base. The paint has been removed. Sturdy and heavy. 26" by 13" by 12". A great children's piece to actually use or for decoration.

**Winning Bid:**

**Viewed**
000067 X

$49.99

**Ended:** 1/25/06
**History:** 1 bid (sold in my store)
**Starting Bid:** $49.99
**Winner:** Riviera, TX

# Oak Children's Chair   #69

## The Story

It is strange, but this chair sold on my grandmother's birthday. She was an Aquarius and I have never known another one like her. She used to say that after she was born, they broke the mold. Isn't that the truth? She would have been 94 years old if she had lived.

I think I was preparing my entire life for her to die, which sounds strange, but when you are that close to someone who is 50-plus years older than you, the fact that they will be gone someday is always in the back of your mind. I would think about it a lot and wonder, what will I ever do if my grandma dies? My brother, sister and I would often discuss it.

My grandma was really the glue that held our family together. She loved her three grandchildren unconditionally. I think sometimes it is hard for parents to do that with their kids, but not so hard for grandparents. If we ever needed a hug, or a shoulder to cry on, or someone to cheer us up or someone to hand us a $20 bill—there she was. I can still hear her saying goodnight to me after I would help her into bed. "Goodnight honey—I love you—see you in the morning." And I would kiss her on her forehead. You just never know when there isn't going to be another morning or tomorrow with those special people in your life.

I am writing this on an airplane headed to Houston, Texas for my connection to Nicaragua, and I have tears rolling down my face. Thank goodness I haven't put on my mascara yet.

So, let's get back to this child's chair and eBay. My grandmother loved antique children's chairs, so when I spotted this one at a garage sale for $5, I scooped it up. I listed it on eBay at auction for $9.99 and I couldn't believe that it didn't sell. I immediately had Mo move it into my eBay store at a fixed price of $49.99. She listed it in my store at 1:32 pm on January 24th. It sold the next day, January 25th, for full price. It barely made it to the next morning. My grandmother kept an oak mission child's chair around because it was one that she especially loved. When Houston started to walk, he loved to sit in it. So, the first thing my grandmother did was ask for a piece of paper and a pen and she wrote, "This oak chair belongs to Houston Wilson, 5/5/97. Originally owned by Cheryl Leaf." She had me tape it on the bottom.

She was going to make sure that Houston got that chair no matter what happened to her when her tomorrows ran out. We still have it, and it still has that scrap of paper taped on the bottom. Houston scribbled on that scrap of paper a few years back and you would have thought he had committed a felony. In my mind, he had.

# #70 EAPG Spooner

**$7.⁰⁰**
Paid
**From:** Thrift store

**Antique EAPG Spooner Flashed Amber Pattern? Vase NEAT!**

### Description:

Antique spooner is very NEAT! I believe this is a spooner or it could be a celery vase. It is 6 1/4" tall and 4" across. There are some scratches on the amber flashed portion and there are some tiny dings/nicks on the pattern. EAPG is Early American Pattern Pressed Glass. If anyone knows the pattern, I would appreciate knowing. Nice, heavy and I would guess 1890s.

On January 25-06 The seller added this information:

A very nice friend of mine has let me know that this is a Celery Vase in the Double Arch (also known as Interlocking Ring????) pattern. King Glass co. and US Glass Co. #13024 circa 1892 per McCain.

**Winning Bid:** **$333.⁰⁰**

**Ended:** 1/27/06
**History:** 9 bids
**Starting Bid:** $24.99
**Winner:** Minnesota

**Viewed**
000224 X

## The Story

I love buying EAPG (Early American Pattern Glass) pieces at thrift stores because it is a wide-open game. There is too much research involved for a thrift store pricer, so I can often get a great deal. I picked up this piece that I thought was a spooner (a vase to hold spoons on your dining room table) for $7. I did a little research and could find nothing about it—no pattern name and no manufacturer's name. So I listed it on eBay with "Pattern ?" in the title.

Then I emailed a photo to my friends Elaine and Bill Henderson, who run www.patternglass.com—an amazing website. It is funny, because I definitely consider Elaine my friend, although we have never met in person nor spoken on the phone. We are email buddies, and she has helped me with every one of my books (except the first one).

She immediately emailed me back the information that I added to the description. I couldn't change the listing because it already had bids. Always a good sign! I couldn't believe it when the spooner turned out to be a celery vase (a vase to hold celery on your dining room table) and it sold for $333. What a score! And can you believe that they actually used to have vases to hold celery in the early 1900s? How strange is that?

When I started doing my research for this story, I couldn't find anything out about the double arch pattern or either of the companies that made it. So I emailed Elaine and asked her for more information. She wrote, "How much do you want to know? It is a little known pattern and there is some extraneous info that I can scan and send. But, honestly, no one cares about this pattern...do you really?"

I did care, so I asked her for the scan. "Okay," she told me, "I'll scan it, but it won't make any sense to you. It talks about the mix-ups in early research and there are a ton of reference numbers." Just as she had warned me, it made absolutely no sense to me. She was right—who cares about that stuff? So, I finally emailed her with a photo of the vase and asked the right question..."Why did this sell for so much?"

Here is her reply: "OK!!! Easy! It is amber stained!!!! There are at least three bidders who are falling all over each other for amber stained EAPG! It has nothing at all to do with that little-known nothing pattern except that they probably didn't own a piece in that pattern. These three bidders will also go nuts for ruby stained."

Mystery solved. I emailed Elaine and told her that she rocks! She emailed back to say, "Next time, just ask me what you really need to know." Isn't that the truth?

What we really need to know and remember is to look for antique (1880s) amber and ruby stained pressed glass. It is strange, but I hate amber glass and usually overlook it because I have found that it isn't that collectible—but once again, I am proven wrong.

www.patternglass.com

# #71 Steiff Hansel and Gretel

$2.00/2
**Paid**
**From:** Estate sale

**RARE Vintage Steiff Puppet Gretel 7072/17 Tag Button**
**RARE Vintage Steiff Puppet Hansel Felt Antique DARLING**

## Description:

RARE Vintage Steiff Puppet Gretel 7072/17 Tag Button. She is about 9½" by 8½". Still has the Steiff button and tag on her skirt along with the hang tag on her dress. In good to very good condition. Needs a cleaning. Her hair needs rebraiding. The back of the round tag says, "Mottenecht Durch Eulan Bayer." The tag on her skirt says, "Made in Germany 7072/17." Covering 59% wool, 41% cotton. Excelsiar cotton wool foam rubber PA 55 Mass 73. Darling! I would guess 1950s to 1970s. If anyone knows, I would appreciate knowing. I couldn't find out any information about this puppet. We have the matching Hansel also up for sale in a separate auction.

**Winning Bid:**

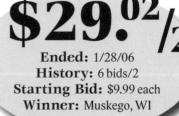

$29.02/2
**Ended:** 1/28/06
**History:** 6 bids/2
**Starting Bid:** $9.99 each
**Winner:** Muskego, WI

**Viewed**

000063 X

# Steiff Hansel and Gretel  #71

## The Story

I was at an estate sale and in a corner of the room was a plastic bag filled with older stuffed animals. I had a hunch that there would be a Steiff animal in that bag. Sure enough, I found these two Steiff puppets, one still with the Steiff button in the ear. I paid $2 total for both of them.

I had just finished reading *Think and Grow Rich* by Napoleon Hill. It is an older book, but I just discovered it, and now I recommend it to everyone. Hill's comments on success have really stuck in my mind.

He claims that for most people, success doesn't occur until they are in their late 40s, 50s and 60s, because most of our earlier years are focused on finding a mate, having children, and maybe just having fun.

Wow! I didn't feel too bad after reading that. Since I started writing my eBay books, I have invested a lot of my own money in my writing career. Self-publishing and self-promotion is not cheap. I used all the money I inherited from my grandmother, plus I have taken out second mortgages on both of my homes.

Selling on eBay pays my day-to-day bills, but my book business has relied on borrowed money to grow. One thing that my parents say about me is that I am tenacious and never give up. They both tell me that they would have given up years ago. I learned this "stick-to-it-ness" from my grandmother.

My grandmother started her own antiques business when she was 37 years old but it took her until her 60s to become really successful. Some of the first products that she carried in her store were Steiff animals.

Steiff was founded in 1880 in Germany by Margarete Steiff, who had been diagnosed with polio in her teens and spent the remainder of her life in a wheelchair. This did not stop her from enjoying her life to the fullest—much like my grandmother, who lived the last twenty years of her life in a wheelchair and never complained. At the age of 33, Margarete began making and selling felt animals. The first one was an elephant that was meant to be used as a pincushion.

Steiff began to achieve some large-scale success in 1903 for its legendary Steiff 55 PB teddy bear (named for Teddy Roosevelt). "55" was for 55 centimeters, "P" for plush and "B" for jointed. It was at this time that the Steiff company began using mohair to make its products more unusual, and, starting the following year, every Steiff animal left the factory with a button in its ear. By 1907, when Margarete was 60 years old, the company became world-famous, manufacturing 974,000 bears that year.

It was a long and hard road for Margarete—the same road my grandmother traveled and that I am still traveling. Never give up on your passion. My two Steiff puppets ending up selling for almost $30 and helped to pay my living expenses. My "stick-to-it-ness" and my book business is finally starting to take off and I have been able to pay down some of my huge debt. It is a wonderful feeling!

# #72  Antique Figural Nutcracker

$2.00
**Paid**
**From:** Estate sale

**Antique Wood Carved Figural Nutcracker German Military**

**Description:**

Antique wood carved figural nutcracker German military. 7½" by 2½" by 1¾". Hand carved nutcracker is very interesting. I would date him from the 1880s to the 1940s. If anyone knows anything we would appreciate knowing. He appears to be a military figure—general? He has a cross or X on his helmet. I am also guessing that he is German. In very good condition.

**Winning Bid:**

# $83.00

**Ended:** 1/28/06
**History:** 13 bids
**Starting Bid:** $9.99
**Winner:** Florida

**Viewed**
000092 X

# Antique Figural Nutcracker #72

## The Story

My grandmother loved nuts. Actually, she loved food, but I think nuts were her favorite. She came from a generation of women who didn't care about their weight. Isn't that an amazing concept? It's a tragedy that the women of today are so obsessed with it.

My grandmother was always a little large. She didn't care, and her husband Elmer didn't care either. She loved to cook and would often make cakes and pies and all sorts of goodies. She even designed and made my mother's wedding cake.

When I was a kid and we were driving up to see her, my little heart would start beating in anticipation. I was so excited to see my grandma and grandpa when we finally saw the Sunset Drive/Mt. Baker exit sign.

From the exit it was only about five minutes to her house, and once we pulled into the back driveway, my brother, sister and I would run to the back kitchen door and barge right in. My grandmother would be waiting and we would run into her arms. Behind her was the kitchen and it always smelled wonderful. She would have something baking especially for us. I loved the smell of my grandmother's home—it smelled like love, safety, and goodness all rolled into one.

I have always known what a nutcracker is because there were always some kicking around my grandma's house. She had the lever types, the big bowls with hammers, and the hand-held metal ones, and some of them were pretty fancy!

My grandma always bought nuts in the shell, never the ready-to-eat kind that come in a jar or can.

Nutcrackers of many types have been used through the centuries. The first nutcracker was probably a rock or hammer, but by the 1800s, many elaborate and ingenious types were being made. Those with levers, screws and hammers were the most popular and the more elaborate, the more expensive and collectible they are today. Yes, people even collect nutcrackers!

I found this figural nutcracker carved in the shape of a man at that same estate sale where I bought the Steiff puppets. The seller only charged me $2 for him and I thought he was unique. He was carved in the shape of a military man with a helmet and everything. I guessed that he was probably German.

I listed the nutcracker on eBay with "German military" and "figural" in the title. I was pleasantly surprised when he sold for $83. Wow! Now if I could just smell my grandmother's old kitchen one more time and have her be there to welcome me. We eventually moved the shop in to her old kitchen, and the last time I got to experience her cooking in it was in 1974—but I haven't ever forgotten it or the love that lived there.

# #73 Tonka Toys Brochure

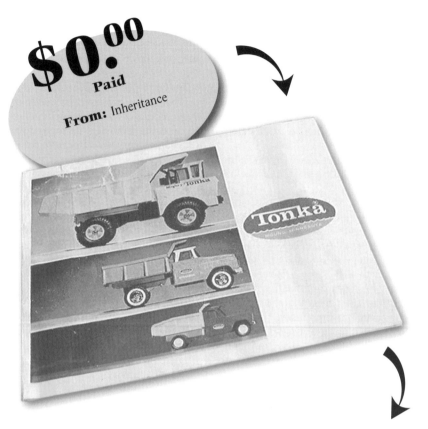

**Tonka Toys Catalog Brochure Vintage VW Bugs 1960s Eames**

### Description:

Tonka Toys catalog brochure vintage VW Bugs 1960s Eames era. This is the cutest little pamphlet. It is from the 1960s to 1970s, I am guessing. Eames era. Has many different toy trucks and cars including the VW bug. So cool. Some wear but in very good condition. 5¾" by 4¼".

Winning Bid:

# $12.00

**Ended:** 1/29/06
**History:** 2 bids
**Starting Bid:** $9.99
**Winner:** Gardnerville, NV

**Viewed**
000016 X

## The Story

I am writing some of these stories on the plane flight back from my trip to Nicaragua with Peter (via Houston, Texas) and I can't stop crying—I'm dredging up too many great memories of my grandmother. "Silly girl," Peter would say to me.

Writing on a plane really works the best for me because I can be totally focused. No telephone, no internet, no radio, no T.V., no kids, no employees, so basically no distractions. I guess I will have to take more trips. Not a bad idea!

I've mentioned it many times already, but my grandmother would never let us throw anything away. This little Tonka pamphlet was tucked into one of the boxes I inherited, and because my grandmother taught us that even the most insignificant piece of paper can be worth something to someone, I decided to put it on eBay rather than recycle it.

My family had moved from Olympia, Washington to Bellingham, Washington between 5th and 6th grades. Just before the start of middle school is not a good time to move an adolescent girl to an entirely new town. Let's put it bluntly: kids can be mean, especially to the new kids. When I was a teenager, I was insecure and battled with my weight, and being "the new kid" made it all the more difficult. It didn't help any that people were constantly saying to me, "You look just like your grandmother."

That always sounded to me like they were saying, "You look chubby," and so my response was, "No, I don't." It probably hurt my grandmother to hear me deny my resemblance to her so emphatically,

but I'm pretty sure she understood and forgave me.

As I grew older and became more confident, I realized that being compared to my grandmother was the highest compliment that I could be paid. During the last seven years of her life, when I was running the store, every time someone said, "You look just like your grandmother," I would say, "Thank you so much!"

I hope that by saying and meaning it in the last few years of her life, I erased the pain I may have caused. Knowing my grandmother, however, she probably never took any of it to heart. She knew what an adolescent goes through and had the most compassion of anyone I know. Besides, she loved me unconditionally.

So back to this scrap of a Tonka brochure that I was selling on eBay. Tonka is most well known for its toy trucks and construction equipment. But Tonka began in 1946 as "Mound Metalcraft" in Mound, Minnesota. Its first product was a metal tie rack that didn't sell well, but when they decided to begin manufacturing metal toys, their future success was sealed. They changed the name to the Native American word "tonka," meaning "great" or "big," in 1955.

This brochure that I sold on eBay only had about 12 pages and was from the 1960s, very close to the time that the company became Tonka. This scrap of paper sold for $12 and I have my grandmother to thank for her Tonka-like "great" lessons in life.

# #74  French Country Table Lamp

$2.<sup>00</sup>

**Paid**

**From:** Garage sale

### French Country Distressed Table Lamp 1940's Darling

**Description:**

French Country Distressed Table Lamp—1940s, darling. This is a great table lamp. The shade is 11" by 7" and is paper. It does have some bends/marks in it. I am guessing that this is 1940s based on the age showing on the base. It does have some nicks. It has a transfer design and some hand painting for the finish. Floral. The shade is newer with *fleur de lis*. It is 6" across at the base.

**Winning Bid:**

# $69.<sup>95</sup>

**Ended:** 1/31/06
**History:** 4 bids
**Starting Bid:** $9.99
**Winner:** Houston, TX

**Viewed**

000102 X

# French Country Table Lamp  #74

## The Story

This lamp was on a table at a garage sale and it was darling. I couldn't tell if it was old or new, but it definitely looked vintage to me. It was at a sale where nothing was priced and I hate that. If I hit one of these sales towards the end of my garage saling day, sometimes I will just leave rather than ask how much items are.

For some unknown reason, I summoned up the energy to say, "How much?" The lady said, "$2," and that was cheap enough, so I bought it.

Upon taking a closer look once I got it home, I immediately thought, "French country" and "vintage 1940s." This was good, because I think that French country is replacing American country as a decorating style. American country is a little old-fashioned and dated (think red checker boards, roosters and animals—slightly unwelcoming and cold but cutesy). French country is more sophisticated and elegant, yet still warm and inviting.

To get an idea of what French country is like, imagine that you are in an adorable little cottage in the French countryside with wrought-iron furniture, bas relief walls washed in butter-yellow paint, and whitewashed distressed chairs. There may even be a primitive farm table you can envision gathering around for a wonderful dinner with friends and family.

This lamp definitely brought all of this to mind, especially with its warm yellow color and rustic floral design featuring *fleur de lis*. The *fleur de lis* is a stylized design of an iris flower. While this symbol has appeared on countless European coats of arms and flags over the centuries, it is most well known and associated with the French monarchy. It is an enduring symbol of France, and in North America it is often associated with areas formerly settled by the French, such as Louisiana and Quebec.

I found it very interesting that the *fleur de lis* was based on a flower. My grandmother loved flowers and gardening. Before she opened her business, her favorite pastime was to putter around in her garden. Her favorite flowers were roses, the rhododendron bushes in front of the shop (which looked more like trees), and the lilac bushes along the side. There was one flower she despised, and that was the lily. She told me over and over again, "Please, no lilies at my funeral." What a funny lady! Every year, she would take a photo of her three favorite (and only) grandchildren in front of those rhodies.

I couldn't believe it when this one lamp ended up selling for almost $70 and was shipped to Houston, Texas. I think it was sold to a business, possibly for resale, so I wonder where it lives today. Maybe the eventual buyer loved flowers as much as my grandmother.

# #75  Midwest Halloween Witch

$1.00 **Paid**

**From:** Church charity sale

### Midwest Eddie Walker Halloween Big Witch Figurine RARE

**Description:**
Midwest Eddie Walker Halloween big witch figurine RARE. Midwest of Cannon Falls—still has the original tag. The Eddie Walker figures are hard to find. 15½" by 5½" by 2½". Witch with a frog and pumpkin. Very cute and in excellent condition. Probably discontinued.

**Winning Bid:**

**$52.97**

**Ended:** 2/08/06
**History:** 16 bids
**Starting Bid:** $9.99
**Winner:** Saint George, UT

**Viewed**
000126 X

# Midwest Halloween Witch #75

## The Story

I love this story because it involves a woman who was like a second mother to me from the time I was two and half until I was five years old. She was out visiting us in Palm Desert in February of 2006. Always a sport, Nedra McColm Schuler got up early to go garage saling with me and my mom.

We lived in Edmonton, Alberta while my dad was a professor at the University of Alberta. We rented a tiny stuccoed house with a yellow roof on "A" street. Right next door lived Nedra and Tom McColm and their kids Kent, Reed and Roxey.

Nedra and Tom quickly became my parents' best friends and their kids were our best friends. I often spent afternoons at the McColm's, and Nedra would feed me my favorite food—pears with cottage cheese. She has such an incredible memory, and to this day can imitate what I would say when she would ask if I would like some more: "Mmmmm nummmm, yes please"!

Those were idyllic days, when there was actually a milkman who would deliver new bottles through a tiny door on the wall by your back porch. It would snow by the foot there and we would spend hours playing out in the snow, only to stop by Nedra's kitchen afterwards for hot cocoa and more pears with cottage cheese.

So on Nedra's latest visit, she, my mom, and I headed out to the sales early on Saturday morning. Nedra calls what we do "junking," and she just can't get over the fact that I actually sell $10,000 worth of merchandise a month on eBay.

We hit a charity sale at the Epis-copal church and I left with several boxes full. One of the items was this Eddie Walker witch that I bought for $1. When we got back into my mom's minivan, Nedra asked me—sarcastically—if I had found any good junk. "Of course," I answered. "Look at this witch. It will sell for a lot of money and it only cost me $1."

Well, she laughed that great laugh of hers (which is quite contagious) and said, "I don't believe it." Later that night, Nedra, her husband Gerald, her brothers, and their wives had a barbecue for us and I brought the witch. I just knew that I needed a photo of Nedra and me with the witch because it was going to sell for big bucks and I would use the photo in one of my books. Check out her look of disbelief and sarcasm.

Eddie Walker is a self-taught artist from Walla Walla in my home state of Washington. She began her carving career in 1989 and now designs for Midwest of Cannon Falls (see story # 56 for more info on Midwest). She is famous for her Easter, Halloween, Thanksgiving, and Christmas figures. Her characters are always smiling and enchanting, just like Nedra.

I knew that an Eddie Walker retired figurine can sell for big bucks. This Halloween witch ended up selling for over $50, and I think I was finally able to wipe that smug look off of Nedra's face when I told her about it! Just kidding! Nedra has a heart of gold and an even better sense of humor. Sarcastic—my favorite kind!

# #76 Oaxaca Tray

$5.00 Paid
From: Garage sale

## Vintage Oaxaca Mexican Pottery Charger Wall Plaque WOW

**Description:**
Vintage Oaxaca Mexican pottery charger wall plaque WOW. This is an awesome piece of pottery. Signed with "Oaxaca" and flowers. It can be hung on the wall and is quite large, 15½", with a tiny lip/rim. There are 15-20 edge nicks/dings but it still looks great. Those types of dings are very common in the older Mexican pottery. I would guess 1930s to 1950s. Blue, green, yellow and brown. It is beautiful.

**Winning Bid:** **$102.50**

**Ended:** 2/08/06
**History:** 9 bids
**Starting Bid:** $9.99
**Winner:** Ingram, TX

**Viewed**
000136 X

# Oaxaca Tray  #76

## The Story

I love traveling to Mexico. My first trip was with my grandmother (of course) on a family vacation in 1978. We visited Mexico City, which was smoggy and overwhelming even back then. I then went to Mazatlan for spring break when I was a sophomore in college and I didn't tell my parents until I ran into a family friend in the airport. Busted!

I first visited Cabo San Lucas with my friend Hank in 1987—can you imagine how cool Cabo was twenty years ago? We stayed at the exclusive Las Palmillas Resort and ate lobster every night for about $400 each for the week. It was crazy.

In the 1990s, my mom bought a timeshare, so we started going to Mexico every year. Puerta Vallarta was my mom's favorite, but sometimes we would go to Cabo or Acapulco. I loved watching the cliff divers. We even took Houston and Indy when they were babies. That was a challenge—I had to bring along formula, cribs, car seats—everything. It is much easier to travel with my kids now that they're older.

I went to Cozumel with Peter in 2001, and I just love that little island on the Caribbean side with its amazing Mayan ruins. It is so beautiful. My kids and I did two mission trips to Tijuana in recent years. My point is that I have traveled extensively in Mexico, but have never been to Oaxaca (pronounced "wah-ha-ka").

Mexico is divided into 24 states or regions, and Oaxaca is the southernmost state on the Pacific coast with about 3.5 million residents. It is one of the largest, yet poorest, regions in Mexico.

The potters in Oaxaca are Zapotecs, Mixes, Mixtecs and Triques—all original Indian tribes. Their work is usually intended for utilitarian purposes such as carrying water, cooking beans, or serving tortillas. The knowledge of how to create this pottery has been handed down from Oaxacan mothers to daughters for about 1,000 years. The pottery is formed without the use of pottery wheels and shaped with simple tools, pieces of gourd, and strips of leather. The pieces are warmed in the sun and fired in open bonfires. The creations are simple and graceful—the work of masters.

Oaxaca is most famous for its black pottery, so this piece that I found at a garage sale for $5 was quite unusual because of all the colors it contained. I have learned in the last few months that certain Mexican pottery sells exceptionally well. I was thrilled when this piece went for over $100 and ended up in a gallery in Texas that specializes in Oaxacan pottery.

Unfortunately, the pottery of Oaxaca is starting to disappear as tin, plastic, and aluminum take the place of clay. I hope that the potters of Oaxaca will be able to keep their wonderful pottery traditions alive by passing them along to their children, just as my grandmother passed her love of antiques, teaching and collecting down to me.

# #77 Hafnia Stainless Flatware

$5.00 Paid
From: Garage sale

## Yamazaki Andersen Hafnia Stainless Eames 5 pc Setting

**Description:**

Yamazaki Andersen Hafnia stainless Eames 5-piece setting. 1 new French hollow knife 8", 1 dinner fork 7¼", 1 salad fork 6½", 1 teaspoon 6⅛", and 1 oval place spoon 7⅛". Very Danish mid-century modern and Eames era in design. Signed "Andersen Japan Yamazaki." In very good condition with some scratches and the usual estate wear. We have a few more pieces up for sale this week in separate auctions.

**Winning Bid:** $158.⁵³/10

**Ended:** 2/10/06
**History:** 38 bids/10
**Starting Bid:** $9.99 each
**Winners:** TN, MI, CO, WA

**Viewed**
000173 X

# Hafnia Stainless Flatware  #77

## The Story

I found these 32 pieces of flatware at a garage sale, and they were marked only $5. It was a very sleek mid-century modern type of pattern, so I scooped it up. It was incomplete, but as you know with eBay, that doesn't matter! I had never heard of the brand Andersen Yamazaki, and it sounded interesting.

When I got married in 1994, one of my favorite aspects of planning the wedding was making appointments in the china departments of all the upscale department stores. At the appointments, we got to fill out our bridal registry. We picked Portmeirion Welsh Dresser as our everyday china, and Reed and Barton for our flatware. Back then, you registered for a five-piece place setting in each of your patterns. The stainless flatware that I found that day at the garage sale turned out to be from a company that claims "quite simply" to have the best quality flatware in the world. Good news for me!

The parent company of Yamazaki is Yamaco. Yamaco, founded in Japan in 1918, is a multi-million dollar raw material trader of stainless steel. In 1930, the founder (Fumikoto) began importing stainless steel from Sweden to use in the production of flatware. He was the pioneer of the stainless steel flatware business both here in the U.S and abroad. Wow! Before 1930, your choices were either silverplate or sterling. Not as useful as stainless for everyday eating.

It wasn't until 1980 that Yamazaki tried to brand its name as a flatware manufacturer here in America. It didn't help that the name was hard to pronounce and felt like a cross between Yamaha and Kawazaki. People often mistook the company for a motorcycle company. I am sure that when I was a department manager in 1985, we carried Yamazaki upstairs in the china department.

Avant-garde, innovative and unique designs are the core of the company, which is known in the retail business as being "fashion forward." The pattern I had purchased was "Hafnia," which is a staple of their line.

Yamazaki has had to change with the times as the idea of the five-piece place setting has begun to go out of style. Yamazaki has shifted 35% of its distribution from the upstairs china department (where a five-piece place setting can sell in the hundreds of dollars range) to the lower level housewares department where a bride can pay $199 for a complete 40-piece set (about $5 per piece).

These 32 pieces of Hafnia that I sold on eBay in ten separate auctions ended up selling for almost exactly $5 each, the typical price per piece in a housewares department. Wild!

I find it sad that the tradition of registering in the china department is falling by the wayside. That was a ritual that I enjoyed so much, in part because it was an older tradition—and a rite of passage that I shared with my grandmother.

# #78  Boy Scout Mineral Kit

**Vintage Eames Boy Scout Rocks Minerals Specimen Kit MIB**

**Description:**
This kit is a great find because not very many of these have survived with all 60 of the tagged mineral specimens intact! Each mineral is tagged with a number from 1 to 60. It has 60 small compartments, each holding a different mineral. The box lid names each one, tells its composition, where to find them and the uses of each mineral. The box is 12¼" by 9¼". Some wear to box and some tape on the lid. Cat. no. 2143 Simple intro to Mineralogy. I would guess 1950s to 1960s Eames-era collectible.

**Winning Bid:**

$27.33

**Ended:** 2/13/06
**History:** 4 bids
**Starting Bid:** $9.99
**Winner:** Garden City, NY

**Viewed**
000072 X

# Boy Scout Mineral Kit #78

## The Story

Peter called me one morning in early February and said, "Have you ever heard of the Phoenix Open?" No, not really. "Well," he continued, "A vendor has sky box seats that we can use—do you want to meet me in Scottsdale?" "Absolutely!" I said, as I thought to myself, "Is the Phoenix Open a car race or a golfing event?"

Turns out that it was a golf tournament. I had never been to Scottsdale. It was such a cute area that once I picked Peter up from the airport we ended up goofing around all day and didn't get to the golfing event until about 2 pm.

Dumb, dumb, dumb. By the time we parked and waded through the millions of people there (well, probably not a million, but it was close), the last group of golfers was on the hole in front of our sky box. We only got to see one golfer hit a shot. Oh, well, it was very interesting anyway. So we had some food and grabbed a few drinks and wandered over to the driving range.

By this time, most of the crowds had left for the day and we were amazed to see J.B. Holmes take some practice swings. He was one of the leaders, but no one really expected him to win. So Peter and I ran over to get his autograph on our programs and on our sky box VIP tickets. Peter also took some photos. Pretty smart! Someday I am going to sell those on eBay because J.B. ended up winning the tournament!

The next morning we went out to garage sales in Scottsdale. It is always fun for me to do this when on vacation. At one sale, I found this really neat Boy Scout rock set for only $5. And, on top of that, I had no cash, so Peter paid for it for me. I love hanging out with Peter because he always carries a lot of cash. Well, he puts the big bills on the outside and a ton of ones inside to impress me. Silly boy.

My brother was a Cub Scout and I was a Campfire Girl. I came across a photo of my brother in his Boy Scout uniform the other day and it freaked me out because he looked just like Houston. I immediately scanned the photo (okay, I admit it—I took a digital photo because I don't have a scanner) and sent it to Lee to show him the resemblance—the big cheeks and round face—all inherited from our grandma Cheryl Leaf. He emailed back to say, "There is absolutely no resemblance between Houston and I." You be the judge.

The Boy Scouts were founded on February 8, 1910, almost 96 years to the day before this kit sold on eBay for $27.33. The Scouts have three specific objectives, called the "aims of scouting." They are character development, citizenship training, and personal fitness. The three specific objectives for my "aims of eBay" are quite similar. They are to be honest and of good character, treat all customers with respect, and have fun!

# #79  McGraw Silverware Chest

**$0.00** Paid

**From:** Antique store (Free with flatware)

**McGraw Flatware Storage Cabinet Silverware Chest Box**

**Description:**
McGraw flatware storage cabinet silverware chest box. Vintage and very nice. This says, "Tarnish proof Silverware Chest McGraw Box Co." Light wood with a drawer. In very good to excellent condition. 14¾" by 11¼" by 5½".

**Winning Bid:** **$46.00**

**Viewed**
000045 X

# McGraw Silverware Chest   #79

## The Story

When you work for a large corporation that pays you while you are on jury duty, it is awesome. You get to miss work and serve your country! Can it get any better than that? The last time I did jury duty was when I lived in Los Angeles and worked for the May Company. It was 1987. I went to the Santa Monica courthouse every day for ten days and was never chosen for a case. I got to leave each day about 1:30 and I hung out at the beach every afternoon. I was living the good life!

When I lived in Bellingham, I would get called to serve, but I was always released when I sent in a letter stating that my grandmother relied on me for her nursing care.

Well, here in California today, things are different. It is very hard to get released by mail. You have to show up for the first day and then you can plead your case. So, on the day that this chest was selling on eBay, I was at the Indio courthouse waiting to see if I would be released. I was really nervous to see what would happen, because for me to miss ten days of work would have been disastrous.

Finally, I was in the courtroom and the judge was explaining that it is very rare for him to ever release anyone from their civic duty of jury service. He asked those of us with a reason to be released to please stay put while all of those willing to serve filed outside. There were about 25 of us left in the room, and one by one we had to stand up and plead our case. I stood up and I was actually so nervous I was shaking.

If I were retired, my kids were grown, or I had an employer that would make up the lost income, I would have been honored to serve. Unfortunately, I am not at that point in my life. I explained to the judge that I am a single mother and that ten days of lost income would affect my ability to provide for my children. I was also writing *Money Making Madness*—the 2nd in this series—and I explained that it was due to my printer in two weeks; I would never be able to honor my commitments if I missed ten days of work. I was stressed.

After everyone spoke, the judge announced the names of those who could leave. It was so strange. People with amazing excuses—people with vacations planned and plane tickets purchased, other self-employed people, students with papers due or exams to take —were told that they had to serve. Luckily, I was released.

So, when I got home from Indio I was surprised to see that this flatware chest had sold for almost $50! The best part of this story (besides the fact that I got out of jury duty) was that I had bought this chest in Bellingham in an antiques store. I wasn't thinking about the chest when I bought it (for $55); I was actually focused on the 70-piece set of silverplate flatware that came inside it. I sold the flatware at a good profit, and the chest itself just about covered the cost of the whole investment. Just remember that selling these chests can sometimes pay for the flatware sets they contain. Now that is justice!

# #80  Two Art Pottery Tiles

## Eames Mid Century Harris Strong Ein Reb Art Tile Israel Flying Fish Poole Blue England Carter Art Tile Framed

### Description:

Vintage Ein Reb art tile Israel. Super neat tile is very mid-century modern and Eames era in design. A very fun piece. With three unique individuals—children? Cobalt blue, red/orange, white and blue. 6½" square, tile is in a frame. Signed "An Ein-Reb Art Ceramic Hand Crafted in Israel." I am guessing that this is a Harris Strong piece in very good to excellent condition.

Poole art tile is neat. There is some crazing but no chips no cracks. 7" square. Signed "Carter Tiles Made in England 56." The back of the tile is white; on one edge it says "Carter Tiles" in raised letters and on the opposing edge it says "Made in England" (also in raised letters). The "56" is on another edge.

**Winning Bid:**

**$57.⁰⁰/2**

**Ended:** 2/28/06
**History:** 8 bids/2
**Starting Bid:** $9.99 each
**Winners:** NJ, VA

**Viewed**
`000082` X

# Two Art Pottery Tiles   #80

## The Story

Throughout the centuries, since 3,000 BC, palaces and houses alike have been decorated with tile art. Think about all the uses for tiles: around fireplaces, as tabletops, as backsplashes in the kitchen and bathroom, to line the tub and even on the floor. It is no wonder that the most rare and beautiful of these tiles have become very collectible.

Utilitarian roof tiles are not very collectible, but small art pottery tiles made by famous makers such as Rookwood, Weller, and Wedgwood can sell for big bucks. I am not kidding—we are talking thousands of dollars in some cases.

When thinking about tiles, I remember my grandmother's amazing fireplace. I am still just sick about the fact that we sold her home which housed the antique store. If there had been any way financially for me to keep it, I would have done it. I dream about the house a lot and wonder what else I could have done so that we wouldn't have had to sell it.

My grandmother imported a fireplace mantel from England in the 1960s, and this became her fireplace. She loved it and the tiles that surrounded it, and many a day I would come in to find her sitting in front of it and burning her paper garbage. No shredder for her—I doubt she even knew what one was—and by burning her important paperwork, she ensured that there was no threat of someone getting her important personal information.

I very clearly remember one day that I was cleaning out a cupboard in her house. I found a pile of letters all wrapped up with a ribbon. I quickly saw that they were all sent from Elmer Leaf to Cheryl Sussex at her sorority, Kappa Kappa Gamma, and they were dated in the 1930s. I thought, "Wow, these are going to be great to read, but first I better show my grandma." I took them in

to her and she looked at them and was extremely silent, and my grandmother was never quiet. My grandfather, Elmer, had been dead for over 25 years.

I said, "Grandma, may I please read them?" "No," she replied, "These are too hot to handle." She went to start a fire. I remember that day just as clearly as I remember what happened this morning. She sat in front of the fireplace and read each one, and when she finished she would throw it into the flames. She had huge tears rolling down her face the entire time.

When she was done, I think she regretted burning them as much as I regretted her burning them. I kept telling her, "I can't believe you did that." She did save one little cardboard book of love notes from my grandfather, and she gave it to me. I still have it on a shelf in my bedroom to remind me that there is such a thing as true love.

So, because of my grandma's fireplace and the tiles around it, I know to buy tiles when I see them. I picked up both of these tiles for $1 each on the same Saturday at two different garage sales.

One was from England (like her fireplace mantel), and one was from Israel. The English tile sold for $26 and the Israeli tile for $31. I was very pleased with my $55 profit that day. I am not pleased with myself for selling my grandmother's home, and even less pleased with myself that I didn't at least take the fireplace mantel and tiles with me to put into one of my homes—to remind me of my grandmother and her love.

# #81  Antique Traveling Scale

$0.00 Paid
From: Inheritance

**Antique 1800s European Balance Traveling Scale RARE!**

## Description:

Antique 1800s European balance traveling scale RARE! This is the most awesome piece! It belonged to my grandma and was in her personal collection. She loved little boxes and scales. I believe that it is European. There are no maker's marks anywhere. The top of the box is etched or wood burned with an ornate design. The scale has double pans but is missing the original chain and the weights. It needs some repair—adding the chain, etc. There is a crack in the wood on the back side. My guess is 1800s to 1870s. Such a neat piece! Measures 5½" by 2¼" by ⅞". The wooden case has the neatest old hinge.

Winning Bid:

**$56.00**

**Ended:** 2/28/06
**History:** 2 bids
**Starting Bid:** $49.99
**Winner:** Burlingame, CA

Viewed
000042 X

# Antique Traveling Scale  #81

## The Story

Once again, I am writing these stories on a plane. I am still crying from the last story I wrote. I literally cry like a baby when I remember certain things about my grandma—what in the world do the airline people think?

I often wonder if my stories make other people sad, too, or just me. What I have learned over the years is that even though I worshipped my grandmother, not everyone did. There were even some people (God forbid) who didn't like her. I guess not everyone can get along with everyone else. So, I am just explaining that I looked at her through rose-colored glasses and that even though she sounds like a saint, she was human, just like the rest of us.

I inherited this antique scale from her. She loved and collected scales. This scale eventually made into the store priced at $145. It was only in the store for the last six months before we went out of business, and at 70% off, it could have been purchased for $43.50. Obviously, it didn't sell.

When I think of scales, I remember the jewelry scale that always sat on the counter in the shop. It was a balancing scale (like this one) that used weights to measure jewelry. My grandmother used it for pricing and buying items. I don't know why that scale made such an impression on me; maybe because it was so hard to use. The scale calculated weight according to the metric system, so you had to translate to ounces. And you had to balance it just right. I just

don't have the patience for those types of scales, but my grandmother did.

She loved that scale, and over the years it took quite a beating. Weights would be lost and replaced with anything that could match the lost piece's weight. I remember using paperclips and quarters. One day the balancing mechanism came off, and we had to tape it all to the base. I am guessing that all in all, we used that scale every day for twenty years.

When I bought the remaining inherited boxes from my brother, I was thrilled to find my grandma's jewelry scale in one of the boxes. When I unpacked it in my garage, I discovered it was now in even worse shape then ever. I have yet to put it in my office on a shelf (where it belongs), but it still sits in my garage high up on a box so that I can see it every day when I get in my car. Strange but true.

When I listed this scale that was in the same horrible condition as mine, I had high hopes. This one was very old, but was missing the chains and the weights. Antique scales with the weights and chains intact can sell for a ton of money. Even in "as is" condition, this one sold for $56! Yipppeee! Notice that I started the auction at $49.99. My sentimentality had kicked in, and if no one wanted to give me $50, I would have kept it on the same box in the garage with my grandmother's scale and started a collection—or a shrine to her—however you want to look at it.

# #82  Two Pairs Roller Skates

$30.⁰⁰/2
Paid
From: Garage sales

**Nike N Dorfin In Line Skates Roller Blades NIB Size 7 8
Chicago Roller Rink Skates Black Mens Size 12 NIB NICE**

### Description:

These awesome skates were worn once or twice. They look great. Nearly new in box. The box says "N-Dorfin-6" and "Size 7 or women's size 8 or UK size 6 and Europe size 39.0." I think they are unisex. R width style 1022233. Orange gray and black. Very sleek and hip. Top of the line. Very expensive originally. With the original paperwork. These will be shipped in the Nike box—just so you know in case you are buying them for a gift.

Chicago Roller Rink Skates Black Men's Size 12 NIB CRS405 style. Men's rink skate has rink-style tigerion boot with speed toe stop. 58 mm wheels for in- or outdoor use. In great condition. There is wear on one of the wheels. Almost new in box, were worn once outside.

**Winning Bid:** $170.⁵⁶/2

**Ended:** 3/06/06
**History:** 45 bids/2
**Starting Bid:** $9.99 each
**Winners:** UK, FL

**Viewed**
000167 X

# Two Pairs Roller Skates   #82

## The Story

My dad was in town to help me with the kids and to celebrate his birthday. He is an awesome dad and grandfather and an even greater person, although we often butt heads. I think the reason is that we are far too similar. But I love him dearly.

So, one Saturday morning, my mom and I were heading out to garage sales and he said, "Here is $20 I want you to invest for me—better odds than Vegas." No kidding. So, the entire morning I fretted about what to spend his money on. I finally decided that I would look for manly sporting items, even though I typically shy away from things like that.

Well, at one of the sales there was a practically new-in-box pair of Nike rollerblades for $30. Not in my budget, but I had that $20 from my dad burning a hole in my pocket. I offered $20 and the sellers finally agreed to take it. Mission accomplished.

Later that day at another sale, I found a pair of Chicago roller skates for $10. The man told me that he had worn them once and crashed, and he would never wear them again. I understand that train of thought. On my second date with William (my ex-husband), we went roller blading. William is an amazing athlete, but you should know that I am not the most coordinated person in the world. I went out and bought brand new rollerblades and all the protective gear that goes along with them. I was ready!

We started out down a huge hill, and I couldn't stop. There was a lot of traffic at the end of the hill and I was petrified that I was going to get hit by a car. I turned as much as I could and ran right into a huge embankment. It was painful and humiliating. I haven't rollerbladed since I got divorced. Smart move.

I listed both of these roller skates on eBay at the same time. The history of roller skates is amazing. In 1760, a London inventor, Joseph Merlin, attended a masquerade party wearing his new inventions, metal-wheeled boots.

He wanted to make a grand entrance, so he rolled into the party while playing the violin. He had forgotten to add brakes to his invention, though, so he crashed right into a mirrored wall and shattered it. Some entrance into society!

Over the years the roller skate has evolved from the parallel variety of wheels to those in a straight line. The in-line skate of today was developed by two brothers from Minnesota who wanted to be able to practice hockey off of the ice. The Olson brothers founded Rollerblade in 1983.

So, on that one day in March, I found both old and new types of skates. The Nikes sold for the most, at $104.56, and I thought my dad would be thrilled to have a return of over 400% on his investment. The old fashioned skates sold for $66 and a 6.6-to-one return. My dad's return was way better than it would have been in Vegas. But my dad, being the gentleman that he is, said that he wanted me to keep the money to help out with the kids. My roller skating crash from years ago didn't lead to any bad luck, only blessings—my kids, my friends and my family.

# #83  Blue Cloisonné Box

**$3.00** Paid

**From:** Thrift store

## MOD Covered Cloisonné Antique Cobalt Blue Box NEAT

**Description:**
MOD covered cloisonné antique cobalt blue box NEAT. This is such a neat piece. It is a navy blue or cobalt blue with circles of décor. Quite MOD and fun in design. I would guess 1930s and Chinese. 3¾" by 2⅝" by 1⅞" and in excellent condition.

**Winning Bid:** **$103.50**

Ended: 3/23/06
History: 8 bids
Starting Bid: $9.99
Winner: Elkton, FL

**Viewed**
000072 X

# Blue Cloisonné Box  #83

## The Story

My grandmother loved Lawrence Welk. Every Sunday night from 7 to 8 pm, it was quiet time. How many evenings did Lee, Kristin, and I have to sit silently while the family watched this show? I thought Lawrence Welk was soooo boring. I just didn't see his appeal. A-one and a-two and a-three... by the way, $3 was what I paid for this cloisonné box.

My grandmother loved cloisonné and anything my grandmother loved made an impression on me. Because of this I always pick up cloisonné when I see it for sale. But, I have to admit, it never sells for very much unless it is Japanese. And this box was a Chinese piece.

But just because my grandmother loved something doesn't mean that it will sell for a lot on eBay, or even that it is a good thing. But you all know how I feel about my grandmother, so I keep buying cloisonné, and this piece was a bargain.

Even though my grandmother was the most influential person in my life, that doesn't mean that we always got along. In fact, when we argued (which was rare), it would be very serious. I was the only person in the ENTIRE family who would stand up to her. If I

thought she was wrong or was making a mistake, I would tell her and I would stand my ground.

I wouldn't back down and neither would she. I think that is why she respected me so much. I was not, and never will be, a "brown noser." I remember one summer while I was in high school, we got in such a HUGE argument that I didn't help her at the summer antique shows in Seattle or Portland.

The strange part of this is that I have no idea what the fight was about—probably something minor—but it was perceived as a serious slap in the face by my grandmother. However, I was learning to become an adult and assert my independence. I dread the day that Indy and Houston do the same.

So, I paid $3 at my thrift store for this cloisonné hinged box. I know that hinged boxes can do well and I also thought that the design—mod circles that reminded me of the Eames era—was very atypical for a Chinese piece. Quite a few people also thought that it was rare because it got eight bids and ended up selling for over $100! Thank you, Grandma, and thank you Lawrence Welk...a-one and a-two and a-three...Quite a return on only a $3 investment!

# #84  Bronze Whale

$131.<sup>45</sup>

**Paid**

**From:** Gumps pallet

**Bronze Heavy Amazing Whale Sculpture Glenn Heath 2005**

### Description:
This is an amazing large and heavy carved bronze piece. I love this piece. It is 8¼" by 1¾" by 3½" and signed "2005." In excellent condition. These Glenn Heath animal sculptures are usually only available in a limited edition. This whale has an amazing patina and look in his eyes. I understand that this is a limited edition piece but all it has as a signature is the year. In excellent condition.

**Winning Bid:**

$249.<sup>00</sup>

**Ended:** 3/28/06
**History:** 1 bid (sold in store)
**Starting Bid:** $249
**Winner:** Honeoye Falls, NY

**Viewed**
000322 X

# Bronze Whale  #84

## The Story

This story is so weird. Weird is one of my favorite words, so let me digress. I used to tell my grandmother all the time that she was "so weird," and because she was "so weird," that made her young. I told her that she was "weird and not old." How can you be weird and old? Not possible. Weird to me is a great thing, and it really just means unique. I loved calling her weird, and she loved it when I called her that.

So back to our weird story, every time that I look at something in my eBay room, touch it, or think about it…it sells. It is the strangest phenomenon. Time and time again it happens. It must be all about positive energy and imagining the good, because when you imagine the good, the good happens.

So, I was trying to explain all of this to my kids. I showed them a few things that had sold out of the eBay room that we had just touched. Mo and I explained that we thought they had sold because of our positive energy. So Houston and Indy, being the wonderfully thoughtful children that they are, said, "Mommy, Mommy, what can we touch in the eBay room to help make it sell?"

I said, "Let's have you touch the most expensive item." One thing you should realize about me is that I am not stupid! The most expensive thing that I had on eBay at that time was a bronze whale sculpture by Glenn Heath. I had bought it on that Gumps pallet from days gone by and paid over $100 for it. It was listed in my store at $249.

Glenn Heath is a well-known sculptor who works in a variety of media, including bronze and soapstone. His sculptures of animals are displayed all over the world by collectors who appreciate the way Heath seems to capture each animal's unique personality and reveal it through their warmly expressive eyes. Heath's subjects vary in size from small (cats, owls, fish) to huge (whales, hippos, and rhinos).

But back to my whale. Houston and Indiana made the biggest and silliest ritual out of touching him. They both stroked his back and then petted him for about five minutes, chanting, "Sell, sell, sell" until we finally put him back on the shelf. The whole time we were all cracking up. And I was looking at them with such love and wonder. What amazing kids to want to help me so much with my business!

It turned out to be not so funny. Because, literally three weeks later, it sold. Okay—it didn't sell immediately after their ritual, but it had been in my store for over seven months. Amazing and WEIRD—you have to admit that!

# #85 Baccarat Shell

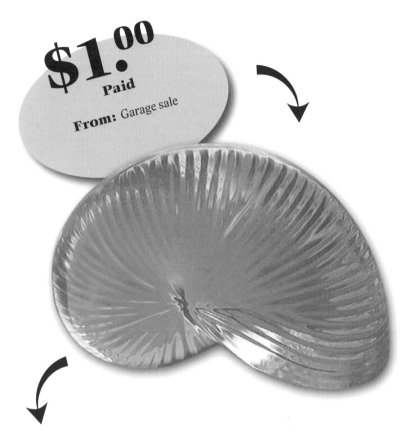

**$1.<sup>00</sup> Paid**

From: Garage sale

**Baccarat Signed Green Nautilus Shell Paperweight France**

### Description:

This is a beautiful piece that is signed "Baccarat." Signed with both "Baccarat" in an etched circle on the base and the script "Baccarat" on the side. 2½" by 1½" by 1". In excellent condition. I believe that they are not making these anymore.

**Winning Bid:** **$62.<sup>14</sup>**

**Ended:** 4/08/06
**History:** 9 bids
**Starting Bid:** $9.99
**Winner:** Lubbock, TX

**Viewed**
`000122` X

# Baccarat Shell  #85

## The Story

My mom and I read about a sale in a community that we had never been to before. You see, most of the homes here in Palm Desert are in gated developments. So, the majority of homeowners are only allowed to have garage sales once a year when their entire community has the sale. We always find great items when we haven't been to a specific sale in previous years.

We arrived a little bit before the published starting time. There was a cute older gentleman (everyone out here is older!) at the gate passing out maps. The map had arrows to indicate which way to drive. Well, my mom and I are no dummies, and we immediately drove in the opposite direction. Why fight the crowds?

But first, we stopped at all the tables set up in front of the clubhouse. As we got out of the car, we ran into Mr. Carroll, Houston's second-grade teacher. We love running into Steve Carroll (a fellow garage saler)—it always starts our day off right. After saying hello, I picked up this shell from one of the tables.

I couldn't see a signature on it, but do you know how a piece of quality glass just feels like a piece of quality glass? And junky glass feels junky. My grandmother always said, "If it was garbage when    it    was made, it will be garbage in the future." I think that still holds true for certain items. But, when things like cereal boxes from the 1970s are selling in the $500 range, I have to throw out my grandmother's advice. I don't want to throw out the baby with the bath water, though. That would mean that I threw away something valuable with something not wanted. So, I will keep my grandmother's good advice when it applies to glass and throw it out when it applies to cereal boxes and other junk!

I only paid $1 for the shell paperweight, and when I got it home in better light I could see its two Baccarat signatures. I had known it was good from the feel—amazing! Baccarat is a very famous French crystal glass company founded in 1746 in the town of Baccarat (hence the name). Baccarat is famous for its perfume bottles, barware, and chandeliers (see #57 in *Money Making Madness*).

I was thrilled when this tiny piece of glass in the shape of a nautilus shell sold for $62.14. Julia, who purchased it, didn't buy it because it was Baccarat, but rather because she collects nautiluses and fossil ammonites. Just what exactly is a nautilus? And what in the heck is a fossil ammonite?

A nautilus is a soft-bodied marine animal with a spiral shell. It is thought to be a descendant of the ammonite (now extinct) and is sometimes referred to as a "living fossil" because it has helped us to understand how ammonites lived.

Ammonites    inhabited the world's oceans about 65 million years ago and now appear as fossils in marine rocks. Ammonites are used to help index and date rocks.

Well, now I am completely confused so will end this story here.    This is the reason I hated science—I just don't get it. However, I do understand that a piece of Baccarat crystal in the shape of a shell will sell for big bucks on eBay!

# #86  Gallant Chess Set

## RARE Gallant Knight Chess Set Pieces Eames Gothic Djaya

### Description:

This is an amazing Gallant Knight chess set, complete with 16 pieces for each side. No board, but there is an antique/vintage wooden box. They are so awesome! They are some type of heavy, substantial metal; one side is silver and the other copper. The felt storage bags say, "Gallant Knight Presents Contemporary Gothic Chessmen designed by Djaya" (I think it says Djaya, but could be Diaya or Djaga). Very mid-century modernistic abstract and sleek. The epitome of Eames era. I would date this set to 1950 to 1960. In very good to excellent condition with a few slight dings; there is one piece with a little bit of wear. The woman I bought this from said her husband had purchased it years ago and that it was very expensive. He may have added felt to the bases; there is felt inside the box. The wooden box measures 7" by 3¼" by 16".

**Winning Bid:** $515.00

**Ended:** 4/08/06
**History:** 24 bids
**Starting Bid:** $49, $399 reserve
**Winner:** Laredo, TX

**Viewed**
000367 X

# Gallant Chess Set  #86

## The Story

I bought this at the same community sale where I got the Baccarat shell. The woman selling it was older (I didn't need to say that, did I?) and so darling. Anyway, she had this set priced at $100. I won't usually take such a risk without doing some research. However, it was 8 am and my brother would definitely not be awake to call for advice. I told her how beautiful I thought it was and asked if she would consider taking $80 for it. She said yes!

I listed it immediately when I returned home with a $399 reserve. I wanted to test the waters without giving it away. It ended up selling while we were at a baseball tournament exactly one week later for $515. What a score! This one wasn't a bunt—it was a home run!

It seems like every weekend in the spring we are away at baseball tournaments. My dad flew in two weeks later on Friday night, April 21st, to attend a San Diego tournament with us. We had the car packed that Saturday morning and were all climbing in when my sister Kristin called. Her water had broken and the baby was coming two weeks early.

Oh my gosh! We all started panicking. Who should fly home to Bellingham? Who would be there when the baby was born? Who would take my kids to the tournament in San Diego? Could I miss one of my son's tourna-

ments? ABSOLUTELY, for my sister's baby!

We finally decided that since my dad hates hospitals and had just arrived from Bellingham, my mom and I would fly up. We quickly got plane tickets and reserved a rental car and were on a flight by 5 pm that evening. What a whirlwind!

We didn't go to the hospital when we arrived late that night, but were there by 9 am the next morning. Kristin finally had her baby boy, Zachary, at 8:39 pm, after twelve hours of hard labor. I am sure Kristin was glad that her mom and sister were there.

My mom and I stayed the entire week and helped clean and decorate her house. The first thing we did was go to Costco and buy her five of those huge baker's racks like I use in my eBay room. She had no storage. My good friends Audrey Mortensen and Jo Dallas even came over a couple of nights to help. We felt like we were back in the shop designing displays.

We even went to garage sales (can you believe it?) on Saturday and found her a glider rocker, the perfect blue rug for the floor in the nursery and a lot of other things that the house needed. The money I made on the chess set all helped to pay for it. It was a whirlwind week, but so much fun—and our family had a new baby to love!

# #87 Six Majolica Fruit Plates

$12.⁰⁰/6
Paid
From: Garage sale

## Strawberry Majolica Plate Italy Italian Fruit NEAT

**Description:**

Strawberry Majolica plate Italy Italian fruit NEAT. 8⅜". No chips no cracks no crazing. A few nicks. Cabbage or leaf background. We have matching plates up for sale in separate auctions. Others with grapes (2) and apples (2).

**Winning Bid:** $103.⁹⁶/6

**Ended:** 5/04/06
**History:** 16 bids/6
**Starting Bid:** $9.99
**Winners:** IN, MI

**Viewed**
000087 X

# Six Majolica Fruit Plates  #87

## The Story

I had just finished writing the second book in my *100 Best* series, *Money Making Madness*. It was fresh off the press, and you know me (or you soon will). I was already thinking about items that would make it into my third book—the one you are reading!

I was out at garage sales with my mom (of course) and we hadn't found anything that day. I mean nothing. On those days, I have a new saying: "A lotta nada." Which means a lot of nothing. It was definitely one of those days.

In one garage sale, a lady had six of these neat majolica-style plates. They were $2 each and I thought I could possibly turn a profit on them, until I flipped them over and saw the dreaded "TJ Maxx" sticker. Don't you just hate that? I am always turning over supercool items to find that they have a "TJ Maxx," "Ross," or even worse, "Big Lots" original price tag.

I am pretty positive that I can't make any real money with the Big Lots (formerly Pik-N-Save) items, but for some reason, I thought I should start trying Ross and TJ Maxx items. I also thought that by buying these plates and testing them, I could create a great story for book number three!

Since I paid $2 each for the plates, I put them in six separate auctions of one plate each. There were two plates with apples, two plates with grapes, and two plates with strawberries. They were signed "Made in Italy," so I could get away with calling them majolica.

Majolica is very vividly glazed pottery mainly produced in Europe and America. Most pieces are done in bas relief—meaning each piece has raised portions that give it an almost three-dimensional quality.

Majolica is the English version of the Italian "maiolica," and refers only to tin- and lead-glazed ware. The most famous of all majolica (and the most collectible) are the Victorian pieces introduced in 1851 by Herbert Minton at the Great Exhibition in London. He used third-century Middle Eastern glazing techniques on eighth-century Spanish forms, uniting both with the maiolica of Renaissance Italy.

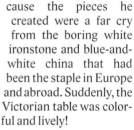

Minton was a true visionary, because the pieces he created were a far cry from the boring white ironstone and blue-and-white china that had been the staple in Europe and abroad. Suddenly, the Victorian table was colorful and lively!

Most Victorian pieces are not signed, but those that are can sell for hundreds (if not thousands) of dollars. The majolica techniques Minton developed are still being used today, and that was what I had—modern majolica—and from TJ Maxx. How modern can you get?

I couldn't believe it when these six plates sold for over $100! And the funny part was that the two strawberry plates sold for the most—one for $26.55 and the other for $27.45—for a grand total of $54. Go for the strawberries when you are out and don't ever turn up your nose at a TJ Maxx or Ross sticker. I shop there for clothes—why not for eBay items?

# #88  Leaf Cookie Mold

**$3.60**
Paid

**From:** Garage sale

**Antique Cookie Butter Mold Press Leaf Leaves Grape NEAT**

### Description:
Antique cookie butter mold press leaf leaves grape NEAT. Leaves and butterfly. I would guess 1900s to 1950s and in good condition for its age. 4" by 7.5" by .5". Darling. We have 5 different cookie molds or stamps up for sale. They are all different but I bought them all from the same lady who collected them. Very folk art and primitive.

**Winning Bid:**

**$84.67**

**Ended:** 5/15/06
**History:** 9 bids
**Starting Bid:** $9.99
**Winner:** Austin, TX

**Viewed**
000169 X

# Leaf Cookie Mold   #88

## The Story

It was the weekend before Book Expo America in Washington, D.C., where I would be debuting my newest book, *Money Making Madness,* along with about 160,000 others. There are about that many new books that come out each year. The competition is fierce.

I was out at garage sales trying to get some things listed before I left. I found five cookie molds, and it was apparent that the seller had been an antiques dealer. She wanted a lot of money for her things, but they were all very nice. I put the five molds in a pile and asked how much she would take for the lot. The lady said, "$20." I asked if she would take $18, and she reluctantly said, "Okay."

Cookie molds or presses have been in existence since at least the 1600s. They were originally used to make picture cookies that would tell a story visually at a time when most people were unable to read or write. Wild!

Beautiful, ornate examples of cookie molds were fairly common in European countries where wood carving was a popular folk art; most would have been carved by farmers for their own use. Some cookie molds were even carved from clay and metal. Most of the molds showed images from the farm, the natural world, and the church.

When these same Europeans began immigrating to the U.S., they brought the tradition of hand carving molds with them. The need for these molds was so great that in the nineteenth century, factories began producing them with lathes. Their original retail price was about five or ten cents. Today, these antique molds can sell for hundreds of dollars.

I got the cookie molds listed in auctions that were scheduled to end about the time I would be in Boston visiting my best friend Melanie on my way to the Book Expo in D.C. I didn't have anyone to watch my kids, so my brother and I worked out a deal. I would pay to send Houston and Indy to Disney World for the week if my brother would take them. Everybody was happy!

So life was pretty good. Boston with Melanie was great, Book Expo was a success, and my kids were on their way to Disney World for the first time in their little lives. Yikes! I didn't get to go to Disney World until I was in high school. Kids grow up so quickly these days and want things sooner and sooner. But the way I figured it, the price of sending them was about the same as the price of a sitter for eight days. The kids lucked out!

I lucked out when this one cookie mold with leaves sold for the most of the whole set, at $84.67! I know it is thanks to Cheryl "Leaf." All five molds ended up selling for $143.67, and my kids spent the week in Disney World—where I am pretty sure that they were eating cookies for every meal! Just kidding.

# #89  Bride's Basket

**$25.⁰⁰ Paid**

From: Estate sale

**Victorian Brides Basket Art Glass Insert Pink Satin WOW**

### Description:

This pink bride's basket insert is a beautiful piece. It is an inset or insert for a basket frame. It is 9" by 2⅞". The base that will fit in the frame is about 2⅜" by ¼". I would guess Victorian and in very good condition. No chips no cracks no crazing. There are 12 raised designs on this piece—circular shaped. It is lovely.

**Winning Bid:**

**$69.⁰⁰**

**Ended:** 5/16/06
**History:** 6 bids
**Starting Bid:** $49.99
**Winner:** Linden, PA

**Viewed**
 **000124 X**

## The Story

I saw this piece at an estate sale and it immediately reminded me of my grandmother. For one thing, it was pink, her favorite color. For another, she owned the most beautiful bride's basket in the world, and it sat on one of the marble tables in her living room.

It was pink and purple, hand-decorated, and sat in an amazing silver-plated stand with huge fruit pieces at the handles and nautiluses around the sides! Then, to top it all off, she had an arrangement of 30 antique hand-blown glass tulips inside.

It was and is literally breathtaking. I loved it, and one day she asked me if I would like to have it. Of course! Thank you, Grandma. She put a label on the bottom saying that it belonged to me. With her favorite items, she would ask that we leave them in her house for everyone to enjoy even after she "gave" them to us. By putting my name on the bottom, she made it known that when she was gone, there was to be no arguing about who owned it.

I always dreaded the day she would be gone—for so many reasons. But one was that I thought the four of us (my mom, brother, sister, and I) might fight over possessions and the way the estate was handled. I thought about it a lot, going over all sorts of scenarios in my mind. A quote I love from Samuel Clemens (Mark Twain) goes like this: "I have been through some terrible things in my life, some of which actually happened."

As it turned out, my fears were unfounded. The settling of the estate went way better than I ever could have imagined, but I had already lived the worst in my mind. We were all bonded by our grief and wanted to show our respect to Cheryl Leaf by getting along. Funny how we tend to imagine the worst instead of the best!

So I decided to buy this insert, even though it was marked quite high at $25. I put it on eBay with a starting bid of $49.99 and was thrilled when it sold for $69, just as my kids' end-of-the-year parent-teacher conferences were taking place.

When the auction ended, I had just returned from Indy's conference, where she had received an absolutely perfect report card. Mrs. Paquette said to William and me, "You both make perfect children—you really should have some more." That may be true, but more children for the two of us together is NOT going to happen.

And Houston had done a book report on *Money Making Madness* for his final class project. How cute was that? I will leave you with his final sentence: "My opinion of the book is that it was very heartwarming because every single story I read really made me want to tell people that this was one of the best books ever written by man or woman." And this from a nine-year-old. WOW! I am just sorry that my grandmother didn't live to see them grow up, because they really are wonderful and kind children.

# #90 Violin-uke Dulcimer

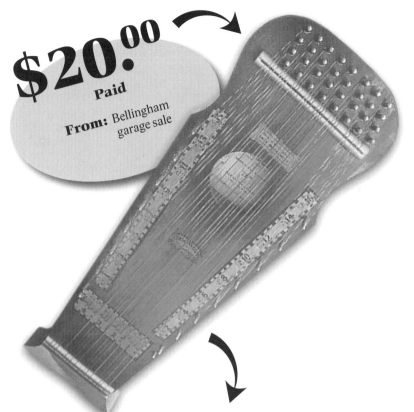

**$20.00** Paid

**From:** Bellingham garage sale

## Original Marx Instrunent Old MIB Violin-Uke Dulcimer

**Description:**

Original Marx instrument old comes in the original box violin-uke dulcimer. Super neat vintage musical instrument comes with the bow. Says, "An original Marx Instrument Conservatory Quality." Violin-uke. Needs cleaning. In good condition. Missing two strings. "Guaranteed 5 years. Patd. app. for. Marxochime Colony." $28.50 when new. Must be vintage—1950s (my best guess).

**Winning Bid:** **$78.77**

**Ended:** 5/16/06
**History:** 6 bids
**Starting Bid:** $24.99
**Winner:** Temecula, CA

**Viewed**
000072 X

# Violin-uke Dulcimer   #90

## The Story

I bought a ton of items to sell on eBay when I was in Bellingham to help with my sister's baby. I had spent a lot of money getting her house ready for the baby—probably close to $1,000—and I wanted to find some great things to offset that expense.

We had gone to an estate sale on 34th street, right by my brother's old house, which is now his rental. That is one thing we all learned from our grandmother—to buy real estate and lease it out. You could always make money waiting for the eventual inflation.

My brother wanted to sell his house about four years ago when it was only worth $125,000. I spent a lot of time on the phone talking him out of taking that step. He thanks me today because it is now worth about $295,000.

As I am sure many of you realize, rentals and renters can be a whole lot of work. My grandmother would get sick of it all sometimes and in a moment of insanity would sell one of her rentals. I am still sick about her selling the house right across the street from the shop.

It not only had a main house, but a smaller rental house out back and a huge warehouse. Oh, I missed that warehouse when I ran the store for her in the 1990s. She sold the entire corner property for only $40,000 in 1988. Today, it is probably worth $500,000.

The warehouse used to be chug-a-rum full (a grandma saying) with old cars, furniture, and boxes stuffed with things she had bought. I loved taking the old key (on a Sussex Motors key ring) across the street with customers to let them poke around. It always fascinated me. I am sure there were things in that warehouse

that would have sold for a fortune on eBay.

Oh, well, back to this stringed instrument that I bought for $20 at that sale three doors down from my brother's rental house. It was made by the Marxochime Colony company and had the original sticker price of $28.50 on it. I had heard about instruments doing exceptionally well on eBay, so kept my fingers crossed. I thought this was going to sell for at least $500 and there was my money back for being a good sister. Not!

What I found out about the violin-uke was that it was a cross between a plucked Hawaiian ukulele and a bowed violin. These were sold door to door in the 1950s on a payment plan. They never were sold for the $28.50 price tag—that was just a marketing ploy to get you to buy it quickly for this special "one-time offer of half off." These instruments were touted as easy-to-master, but many purchasers became frustrated when they couldn't learn to play them quickly and ended up tucking them away in attics, backs of closets, and warehouses!

I guess almost everyone in this country has a violin-uke in a back closet. I am positive that there was one in my grandmother's big warehouse across the street that she sold for NOTHING. Mine didn't bring anywhere near my dream price, but it did earn me a $58.77 profit. Still better than nothing!

# #91 Papier-mâché Masks

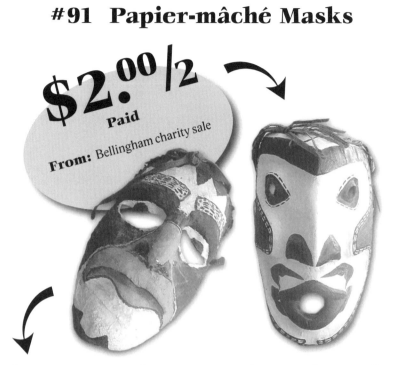

$2.⁰⁰/2
Paid
From: Bellingham charity sale

## Now You Have Eagle Eyes Too Native American Mask Mache Native American Mask Papier Mache Roy Peters 1985 Neat

**Description:**

This mask is really neat. I bought it at a charity sale so don't know more than what is written on the back side. It says, "Now You Have Eagle Eyes, Too Eagle R. Prior Sept. 1991." Native American and made from papier mache. In good to very good condition. Needs cleaning. Some nicks. We have another similar one up for sale. 5¾" by 9¼" by 4½".

Another neat mask that I bought at the same charity sale so don't know more than what is written on the back side. It says "Roy Peters -85-" 10" by 6½" by 5½". In very good condition. Looks to be Native American or Eskimo and made from papier-mâché. We have another similar one also up for sale.

**Winning Bid:** $46.⁴⁷/2

**Ended:** 5/19/06
**History:** 8 bids/2
**Starting Bid:** $9.99 each
**Winners:** CA, WA

**Viewed**
000089 X

# Papier-mâché Masks  #91

## The Story

While we were in town for Zachary's birth, there was a great charity sale in Bellingham one Tuesday (strange). It was held at the Episcopal Church on Walnut street right down from our old shop.

My daughter Indiana had gone to preschool at this church. It was her first school! I still have a darling picture of her on her first day there. She looks so tiny, and she is jumping in the air with excitement.

My mom and I were in line about twenty people back with our empty boxes waiting for the sale to start. Several former customers from the shop were also in line, and said, "Hello, what are you doing in Bellingham?" We were so proud to tell them that Kiki (my sister) had just had a baby.

I bought a lot of stuff that first day, but inquired to see when they would be marking things down. There was a Stangl dish set that I had my eye on but did not want to spend $175, plus the cost of shipping it to Palm Desert. They said that the next day, Wednesday, things would be half price.

So on Wednesday morning I was first in line. Actually, I was about the only one in line. I rushed right in when the doors opened and grabbed the price tag from the dish set and said I would buy it. Then I went to the boutique section and saw these masks. They had been priced at $2 each on the first day, so on that second day they were only $1 each. You can't go wrong with masks for $1, so I bought them both.

I had never seen masks like this. They appeared to be papier-mâché. Most of us know what that is—in fact, Indiana had made papier-mâché balloons in that very same church back in 2001! It is a substance made by mixing wet paper pulp with glue or paste, which is then placed over some type of form and allowed to dry.

Papier-mâché hardens as it dries, and once hard it is suitable for painting. "Papier-mâché" just means "chewed-up paper" in French. Apparently, French workers in London papier-mâché shops did just that—chewed up the paper—to get it ready to use. Gross! However, despite its French name, papier-mâché was actually developed by the Chinese, who also invented paper.

I listed both of these on eBay during the same week. Eagle eyes sold for $24 and the other mask went for $22.47. $46.47 is not a bad return for a $2 investment. Native American masks are very collectible and the majority are carved from wood. I think these sold well because they were unique.

These masks actually looked like they were made by placing the papier-mâché paste right over a person's face. Crazy! I hope they don't try that trick at my daughter's old preschool—or any preschool, for that matter!

# #92 Tiki Furniture Set

**$100.00**
Paid
From: Garage sale

**Eames Tiki Frankl Rattan 6 Pc Sectional Set Chairs WOW!**
**Rare Early 1940's Living Room Set Vintage Hawaiiana!**

### Description:

The lady I bought this wonderful set from sent it over from Hawaii in the 1940s. There are six matching pieces with curved rattan/bamboo. Definitely Eames era and a fun set because the pieces can be mixed and matched to make a loveseat and two side chairs or one very long couch and one side chair. Six pieces total with two armchairs, two middle chairs and two tables. Could be early work by Frankl. No signatures but there are some very old Bekins moving tags on the base of the end table. The pieces are in very good condition for their age. No cushions. Must be picked up or buyer to arrange for shipping.

**Winning Bid:** **$249.00**

Ended: 5/21/06
History: 1 bid
Starting Bid: $249
Winner: Santa Monica, CA

**Viewed**
000233 X

# Tiki Furniture Set  #92

## The Story

I love Trader Vic's. I have loved this bar and restaurant since we used to frequent it at the Beverly Hilton Hotel during college. Strangely enough, I should be at that hotel this evening as I write this story, but I am so behind, I had to pass on a gala event being held there to honor my friends Dean and Shannon Factor. They are receiving an award tonight for their donations to the Covenant House—a charity that helps children.

Oh, well, I can just taste that scorpion bowl drink—the one that came with six straws for sharing with your friends. Those were the days! Trader Vic's has a very interesting history. It was started back in the 1930s (if you can believe that) as a Polynesian-themed restaurant in Oakland, CA, by Victor Bergeron.

Victor Jules Bergeron grew up loving the food business. He lost a leg in a childhood accident, and that loss helped him develop his skill at telling great stories and entertaining his friends. In 1932, with a nest egg of $700, he built a pub across the street from his family's grocery store and called it Hinky Dink's. His crazy stories, strong tropical drinks, and Polynesian dishes made him a popular host.

By 1936, a newspaper reviewer wrote that "the best restaurant in San Francisco is in Oakland!" Vic soon became known as "The Trader," and Hinky Dink's name changed to Trader Vic's. Its South Pacific theme made customers think of tropical beaches, island girls, and surfer boys. It offered a "complete escape," said Trader Vic. This was especially appealing to people during the time the U.S. was getting ready to enter World War II.

Today, Trader Vic's is found in 25 major world locations, including such far-away cities as Beirut and Taipei. The island style, great service, and relaxing atmosphere make Trader Vic's feel like a club without a membership fee. A faux vacation to the tropics!

So, back from my faux vacation, and to the task at hand—finishing this book! I saw an amazing tiki-style set on the grass at a garage sale and I said to my mom, "That is so Trader Vic's-tropical—I love it." It was only $100 and the next thing you know, my mom and I were wrangling everything in the minivan to make it fit in one trip. We are packing pros, and the mission was soon accomplished!

I listed it on eBay the first time with a $499 reserve. I really thought it was worth it, but it didn't sell. If I had had any extra space, I would have parked it in my eBay store and let it wait for the perfect buyer. That wasn't an option, however, so I immediately relisted it with a $249 starting price and no reserve. It sold to a Hawaiiana dealer from Santa Monica, and he drove out to get it.

I do hope that whoever eventually bought this set is enjoying it as much as I enjoy the atmosphere at Trader Vic's. If you ever have a chance to visit a Trader Vic's, I highly recommend it—Scottsdale, Atlanta, San Fran, Chicago, Las Vegas, and Dallas are just a few of the other locations. Cheers to the island life!

# #93 Bread Pan Katzinger

$0.00 Paid

From: Inheritance

## Antique Bread Pan Katzinger 4 Loaves Commercial Tin WOW

**Description:**
Antique bread pan Katzinger 4 loaves commercial tin WOW. Marked "Katzinger 47" and it is very neat. It is rusty, has tarnish and some missing pieces.

**Winning Bid:**

$24.99

**Ended:** 6/07/06
**History:** 1 bid (sold in store)
**Starting Bid:** $24.99
**Winner:** Sulpher, OK

**Viewed**
000035 X

# Bread Pan Katzinger #93

## The Story

Summers working for my grandmother were the best. Well, summers in Bellingham in general were my favorite time of year. FINALLY, the days were longer, the sun shone, and there wasn't so much rain. On those summer mornings I would often get to the shop early to dig into our work. I can still remember the smell of a Bellingham early summer day—it brings back grand memories.

One summer we decided to tackle the old garage in the back of the property. It had been the dumping ground for years and we thought it would make for a great project. It was 1996, and I had just had Houston—he was so tiny. My grandmother would hold him in her wheelchair and I would work. We uncovered so many treasures—and just as much trash!

Our goal was to turn the garage into a "garage sale" space that would be open every day. We put all of our clearance merchandise out there, and on warm summer days, we would slide open the old-style garage door to attract business. Our customers loved it!

Clearance Annex & Parking in Back

It's Like a Garage Sale Everyday!

One of the things that I came across in the old garage was this antique bread pan. It was pretty rusty, but we still thought it was neat, so we marked it $125 and put it into the shop. It was great for display, and we didn't care if it ever sold. We used it in every single Christmas display because it would hold a ton of ornaments.

It was signed "Katzinger" and the company history is quite fascinating. Edward Katzinger was a tinsmith who left his secure $25-a-week job as a master mechanic to open his own business in Chicago in 1888. He called it the Edward Katzinger Co., and it manufactured tin pans for commercial bakeries.

Over the years, the company grew by acquiring 35 different companies. You might recognize the company better by its shortened name, Ecko. They still manufacture a broad line of household products, including kitchenware and bakeware, molded plastic products, and pest control. In the mid-1990s, Ecko billed itself as the leading supplier of metal bakeware and kitchen tools in the U.S.

I had no idea that my Katzinger pan was a very early Ecko bakeware piece. I tried it on eBay at auction for $49.99, and when it didn't sell, I lowered the price to $24.99. It still didn't sell. I moved it into my eBay store at a fixed price of $24.99 in November of 2004. It didn't sell for almost two years, and because it was too big to stay in my eBay room this poor metal pan had to go back to the garage (albeit another, cleaner, newer garage) to wait for a new owner.

The moral of this story is never give up hope, because FINALLY, in June of 2006, this pan was purchased and sent to Oklahoma to live on Ranch Road. I hope it is now residing inside and is through living in garages.

# #94  Pigeon Plate

**Buffalo China Pageant of Pigeons LA Club 1911**

**Description:**
This is a plate from a Pigeon Club in Los Angeles in 1911. What a wild and strange plate. Made in USA, 9½". Says "Pageant of Pigeons Los Angeles Pigeon Club Inc. Champion Plate. Founded 1911." No idea what it was for. No chips no cracks no crazing. Needs cleaning. Gold wear.

**Winning Bid:**

$16.<sup>49</sup>

**Ended:** 6/9/06
**History:** 2 bids
**Starting Bid:** $9.99
**Winner:** New York, NY

**Viewed**
000042 X

# Pigeon Plate #94

## The Story

Okay, this one takes the cake. My grandmother used to say that, and she also used to tell me, "You learn something new every day." Isn't that the truth? I am still so in shock because of my research for this story that I don't quite know where to begin.

As some of you may remember from my first *100 Best* book, I used to show my cocker spaniel Springdale Buffington professionally when I was in high school. My brother, sister, and I were also members of the Dog-gone 4-H Club for quite a few years. We would show our dogs at the Lynden Fair every summer and compete in both obedience and showmanship.

My Buffington was not that smart, but I excelled at showmanship (the way I handled Buffy). My brother and sister's dog, Sundance, was super smart, so they excelled at obedience. The world of dog showing is a strange one, but at least it's familiar to me. I understand the showmanship of dogs.

What I am not grasping is that there is a whole world of professional pigeon handlers, trainers, and racers. I had no idea that this plate was actually a trophy that had been handed out to the champion pigeon at an LA show in 1911. Wild!

Apparently, there are pigeon clubs all around the world as well as pigeon shows similar to the Westminster show for dogs. Pigeons have breed standards for the size and alignment of the head, eyes, beak, neck, body,

Dog show

wings, legs, rump and tail, as well as the bird's overall posture. Conformation classes judge how well a pigeon "conforms" to these standards.

There are also pigeon races where homing pigeons are removed an agreed distance from their home lofts and then released at a predetermined time. The arrival of each bird at its home loft is carefully noted. The yards per minute is calculated, with the winner being the bird with the highest yards-per-minute rate. Pigeon racing was very popular in the 1920s and champions would often have their portraits painted professionally. Imagine stumbling across one of these at an estate sale!

Of course, homing pigeons were originally bred to carry messages over long distances. These messages had to be short so the pigeons could carry them, and important, because the pigeons would have to be carried over land from their home loft to wherever the messages would originate from. Most of these types of messages related to catastrophes and warfare. How incredibly interesting!

Well, back to my grandmother saying, "That takes the cake!" I would say that showing and racing pigeons is the most extreme example of animal showmanship that I have ever (never) heard of! This plate sold for $16.49 and was shipped (not by carrier pigeon, but by UPS) to New York.

# #95 Halcyon Battersea Boxes

**$550.⁰⁰/18**

**Paid**

**From:** Estate sale

**Halcyon Days Battersea Enamel Box Hot Air Balloons NEAT**

## Description:

Halcyon Days Battersea Enamel Box Hot Air Balloons NEAT. Oval hinged box that opens on the end (side). Unusual. 2⅛" by 1½" by 1". Blue with hot air balloon for decor. Says "Look up, not down, look forward, not back." A neat motto. Colorful hot air balloons on the inside. Bilston and Battersea Enamels, England. We have a wonderful collection of Halcyon Days Bilston and Battersea enamel hinged trinket Limoges-style boxes up for sale this week. All are in excellent perfect condition unless noted otherwise.

**Winning Bid: $1,420.⁹⁰/18**

**Ended:** 6/14/06
**History:** 130 bids/18
**Starting Bid:** $24.99 each
**Winners:** OK, CA, WA, LA, UK
FL, ME, TN, MA

**Viewed**
**001704 X**

# Halcyon Battersea Boxes  #95

## The Story

It was two weeks before eBay Live in Las Vegas, and I was out garage saling. There is a certain area of my valley that I typically shy away from because it is quite far and I have never found anything of value there. However, the newspaper advertisement stated that they had Limoge boxes and Royal Doulton figurines.

My mom was back in Bellingham for the summer (too hot here), so I grabbed Indy and we made the 25-minute drive to the sale. We didn't arrive until about 11 am and I thought that the two collections would be long gone. But no! They were still available. Amazing! Probably because the valley gets deserted in the hot 120-degree months. Works to my advantage.

Anyway, there were nine Royal Doulton figurines and nineteen Halcyon Days Battersea boxes. They weren't Limoges, but Battersea— even better! Read story #13 in *Money Making Madness* for more information on Battersea. The seller wanted $100 to $200 for each Doulton and $35 for each Battersea box. That would have been about $2,015 for everything.

So, I asked my favorite question, "How much if I buy everything?" He said that a dealer had offered him $1,500. I told him that it sounded like they were already sold. He said that it wasn't for sure—and that he would rather sell them to me right now at a discount because "a bird in hand is worth two in the bush."

We agreed on $1,250 and I gave him all the cash in my pocket—$200. I told him I had to drive about an hour

round-trip to my bank. I got a receipt for my deposit and off we went.

While exhibiting at eBay Live, I sold all but one of these boxes, bringing in over $1400. And half of my twelve buyers bought multiple boxes, helping to drive up the prices. The box that sold for the most, at $138.49, was a hot air balloon.

What about the box that didn't sell? My dad had flown in to watch my kids while I exhibited at eBay Live. He saw the plate full of boxes in my office and asked me if he could buy one. "No," I said. "They are all listed on eBay and will probably sell for close to $100 each." As he walked out of my office, I thought, "That was rude of me."

I followed him into the other room and asked why he wanted one. It turns out that he collects them and I didn't even know that! I said, "Okay, which one is your favorite?" Even though almost all of them had bids, I thought I could figure something out because Father's Day was that Sunday. My dad grew up without much and never asks for anything. He wouldn't tell me his favorite. I said, "Fine, I will pick it."

He knew better and went to take a closer look. His favorite one said, "I may not be rich or famous but my grandchildren are priceless." I loved it! I quickly got on eBay to see how I could cancel the auction without making any bidders angry. Guess what? It was one of the only boxes without a bid! I quickly ended the auction and I had a wonderful Father's Day gift for my dad! Cool!

# #96  Royal Doulton Figurine

$77.77 Paid
From: Estate sale

**Royal Doulton Figurine Fortune Teller HN2159 2159 RARE**

**Description:**

Royal Doulton Figurine Fortune Teller HN2159 2159 RARE. This is one of the harder-to-find figurines, looks like an older mark to me. "Copyright 1954" with a "1485" embossed in the base. In excellent condition. No chips, no cracks no crazing. We have quite a few wonderful Royal Doulton figurines up for sale this week, including some very hard-to-find ones.

Winning Bid: **$283.60**

**Ended:** 6/14/06
**History:** 16 bids
**Starting Bid:** $99.00
**Winner:** Perth, Australia

Viewed
000229 X

# Royal Doulton Figurine  #96

## The Story

It was our second year exhibiting at eBay Live and we had *great* booth placement thanks to our friend Mark Furrer from Chase Marketing. We love Mark! Our booth was right on the main aisle across from Pink's Lounge.

Mo and I drove in and set up the night before the opening day. We were ready to go. On the first day, it quickly became apparent that we were going to need some extra manpower. Our fortune-telling skills for predicting how eBay Live would go were way off!

We were swamped the entire time. I called my mom and she flew down from Bellingham. Then, in utter desperation for more help, we called my brother to drive out from LA. Our team was intact.

It was a really fun three-day show. We saw the opening address with Bill Cobb and Meg Whitman. One of the best parts was that Davy Jones from the Monkees performed. How fun! We ate a lot of great meals and went to the free Huey Lewis concert on the last night. eBay always goes all out, and it was a blast.

There was even an authors' luncheon where I got to talk with Janelle Elms, Julia Wilkinson, Skip McGrath, and several others whom I had never met. Not to mention all the really neat eBayers we got to meet and greet during the day. I even got to sit down for another fun interview with Griff and Lee. But (unfortunately), no dancing the pogo with Griff this year.

While we were there exhibiting, the Royal Doulton figurine auctions were ending. Royal

Doulton is a world-renowned British company dating back to 1815 that produces tableware and collectibles. The figurine that sold for the most—almost $300—was the fortune teller. I had paid $700 for all nine figurines, and the entire batch sold for $1822.55. I made about $2,000 from that one estate sale. That was definitely going to help pay for my expenses at the show.

At eBay Live the year prior, we had met Ian Clarke, an executive from eBay Canada. Such a nice guy, and he stopped by our booth in Las Vegas to say hello. I mentioned that Meg was going to be signing autographs and asked if he thought I should go. He was shocked that I had never met Meg. He said "Go!" So off I went, grabbing a *100 Best* book for her to sign and copies of both books to give her as gifts.

I took my place in the long (and getting longer) line to wait my turn. I have to admit that I was extremely nervous. Meg Whitman is such an amazing executive and it was going to be an honor to meet her. When I got to the front of the line, I could barely talk and I was shaking. Just perfect! She was more than gracious, even thanking me for all I do for eBay, and we took a photo together. Look at how scared I still look! I have the signed Meg Whitman *100 Best* book on a shelf in my office.

Now if I could just foretell the future about how well this book is going to sell and how many we should print, I would be in business!

# #97  Amen Wardy Jacket

## Amen Wardy Fancy Beaded Jacket Sequin Rhinestone 6 WOW

### Description:

Amen Wardy fancy beaded jacket sequin rhinestone 6 WOW. This is an amazing jacket. This specially embroidered evening attire jacket looks like the design is done by hand...sequin by sequin, bead by bead, and rhinestone by rhinestone. Stunning! Approximate measurements 22" arm length, 22" length from shoulder set-in and 26" from collar. Says, "Do not wash. Do not dry clean. Professionally spot clean only." Size 6 and in excellent condition. Looks never worn. I bought a few very nice pieces from an estate where money was no object.

**Winning Bid:**

**$66.⁰⁰**

**Ended:** 7/1/06
**History:** 3 bids
**Starting Bid:** $49.99
**Winner:** Chula Vista, CA

**Viewed**
000064 X

# Amen Wardy Jacket  #97

## The Story

Let's see, where do I begin? Hollywood or Chula Vista? You may remember Chula Vista from story #65 about the baseball tournament. That is where this wonderful item ended up. And as I write this, I am sitting at the Hollywood Roosevelt Hotel in the Tropicana bar writing my last few stories. Hollywood is where Amen Wardy sold *haute couture*. Small world, isn't it?

Let's get back to this amazing jacket. It was incredibly hot in Palm Desert and there were not very many garage sales. I was out alone (again) because my mom was gone that entire summer, and I was racing down Highway 74 to find a sale advertised in the paper when I spotted a white tent along the side of the road with some signs. It was a makeshift garage sale set up on one of the frontage roads. Strange.

I quickly pulled a U-turn and parked. The lady holding the sale told me that she was selling some expensive clothing for a friend of hers. Clothing that is expensive originally is always good. I picked up a St. John knit dress and this Amen Wardy jacket. I had never heard of Amen Wardy, but for $10, why not? And it was beautiful.

The Amen Wardy reminded me of the expensive beaded jacket that my grandmother bought to wear to my wedding. She spent almost $200 on the outfit, which was a fortune in her eyes. But me and my wedding meant a lot to her. It was the very same outfit that she would eventually be buried in.

I got home and did some research but couldn't find out much of anything about Amen Wardy himself. What did keep coming up was that Amen Wardy was a *haute couture* retailer and sold many glamorous costumes and outfits to the stars of Hollywood. Wow! I thought I might have a piece worth thousands of dollars. Not to be.

Amen Wardy sold only the finest designers at his famous Newport Beach boutique. By spring of 1990, when he opened his new store on South Rodeo Drive, Amen Wardy already had a huge following of dedicated shoppers. Wardy divided his new store into sixteen individual "boutiques," each of which featured clothing from a specific designer or couture house. The quality of Amen Wardy clothing was high, and the prices were astronomical. The Beverly Hills Amen Wardy closed its doors in 1992, but there is still a store in Aspen, Colorado.

I listed this jacket the first time with a $99 starting price. No one bid. I lowered it to a $49.99 starting bid, and it ended up selling for $66. Not thousands, but still a very respectable return. And the beauty of the story—I am in Hollywood today to see the musical "Wicked," and the jacket ended up in another of our favorite places— Chula Vista!

My grandmother is also buried in her favorite place—next to my grandfather.

# #98  Nude on Wood

$3.<sup>00</sup> Paid

From: Estate sale

**Nude Woman Dot Oil Painting Impressionist Vintage Eames**

### Description:

Nude woman dot oil painting Impressionist vintage Eames. This is a great painting on wood. It is either oil or acrylic and I am guessing 1950s Eames era. A larger sized nude woman. Really well done. 17" by 20". Interesting. No signature.

**Winning Bid:**

$33.<sup>99</sup>

Ended: 7/9/06
History: 7 bids
Starting Bid: $9.99
Winner: Cadiz, Spain

**Viewed**
000253 X

# Nude on Wood #98

## The Story

It was deep in the heart of summer and almost my birthday, when I had to haul not one but two of my kids out to garage sales. One at a time is manageable, but both of them together can be trying. Houston especially hates it—to him, garage saling is like shopping, and this boy does not like to shop. Indy loves to shop, but her limit is about three hours. After that, it is meltdown time. I am sure some of you have heard these words: "When are we going home?" "You said only one more sale and we just went to two more sales." "Mommy. . . . "

This one particular sale had been advertised as an estate sale and I should have been there when it opened. There were tons of items, but most of them were being carried out already. I hate it when you arrive at a sale and the streets are filled with people carrying out boxes full of stuff. That is when I get a sinking feeling in the pit of my stomach. Oh, well. There is only so much you can do when you are a working parent.

Inside the house, there was a painting of a nude woman up high on the wall. One of my ecourse students (and eventual boot camper), Linda Lange, had told me about her luck selling nudes on eBay. I grabbed a stool and tried to get the painting down. I almost killed myself. Houston was worried and wondered what in the world his mommy was doing, but he helped me take it off the wall. It was $3, and Houston thought it was gross!

I told him it was going to sell for a lot of money and that is when he became interested. He wanted to invest the $5 that I had given him to shop for himself that day in my

painting. Sorry, buddy—you thought it was gross.

I never dreamed that I was going to be an antiques dealer, author, and teacher. My childhood dream was to be an artist. When I was little, I used to do these wild drawings and paintings that involved making circular forms and then coloring them all in with bright colors. I used to hold art sales in my bedroom when I was about five years old. I would price each piece at five to twenty-five cents and my showings would sell out. I guess I was always destined to be a businesswoman!

Anyway, I got this oil painting on wood listed on eBay and it ended up selling for $33.99. The buyer lived in Spain and that's where we shipped it. 253 people viewed this auction. If you ever find nude paintings, just remember that they are very collectible. They don't even have to be signed. Amazing! It is even worth it to climb up on precarious stools to grab them.

# #99 Hollywood Bike

$50.<sup>00</sup> Paid

From: Thrift store

**Vintage 1968 Hollywood Cruiser Schwinn Bike Bicycle FAB**

### Description:

Vintage 1968 Hollywood Cruiser Schwinn bike bicycle FAB. This is a great vintage bike that I believe to be about 19" to 20" from the middle of the crank to the seat. Has Kenda tires that are flat. They look to be in good condition. I did not attempt to blow them up. It is 30" from the ground to the top of the seat. The seat says, "Mesinger." It will be partially taken apart to ship. It comes with both front and rear fenders. There is some slight rust and dings but in overall very good condition for its age. It needs to be cleaned up. Some wear to the Hollywood name and the fenders. A great retro bike!

**Winning Bid:** **$102.<sup>50</sup>**

**Ended:** 7/9/06
**History:** 23 bids
**Starting Bid:** $9.99
**Winner:** Dillsburg, PA

**Viewed**
000173 X

# Hollywood Bike #99

## The Story

eBay was taking over my life. My living room, my garage, my dining room table, you know how it goes... So, I decided one day in July that it was time to clean house—move out some of those huge items that I had been collecting. The first item to go was this cruiser bike. It had sat alongside my car (when my car actually fit in the garage) for about eight months.

Once again, I was dreaming big when I saw this bicycle leaning against the counter at my favorite thrift store. I have heard of vintage bikes in perfect condition selling for thousands. Without calling my lifeline Lee or even going home to do some research, I said, "I'll take it." Well, I couldn't fit it in my car, so I detached the handlebars and the seat and took them home with me. This was a trick I learned from my grandmother.

Whenever she bought something that she couldn't immediately take with her, she would take a piece that would make it impossible to sell the item to someone else. If it was a dresser, she would take a drawer. If it was a marble top table, she would take the marble piece. If it was a lamp, she would take the shade or the base. Tricky and smart! My grandmother had already paid for the item, but you just never know what can happen while you are away making your plans on how to come back and pick it up.

Well, I eventually got the entire bike home. I did my research and found out it was worth about what I had paid, $50. Not much motivation to list it. If it had priced out at $1,000 in my research, I would have listed it immediately.

Another reason that I hadn't listed it yet was because I couldn't get the handles and the seat back on.

Remember how smart I was to take those pieces off and carry them home so no one else could buy it? In this case, maybe not so bright, since I am not very handy.

So, one day that summer my ex-husband was over and I offered to pay him $5 to put the pieces back together. He did it and I was finally able to list the bike. I started the bidding at $9.99 because I just wanted the thing out of my house. I was really happy when the bike sold for over $100, and the buyer was happy to pay the $59.95 shipping costs.

The only down side was that when it came time to package the bike, Mo and I couldn't get it taken apart again! I don't even remember how we finally managed to disassemble it, but it sat in my living room for a week until we did. Where is a good handyman when you need one?

# #100 Mexican Saddle

**$75.00**
Paid (with horse)
From: Charity sale

## Vintage Mexico Leather 205 Youth Western Saddle NEAT

**Description:**

Vintage Mexico leather 205 youth western saddle NEAT. Super saddle is signed with "#205" and "Hecho en Mexico." Child's, youth, children or kid's size. I believe it is vintage. There is some wear to the leather. The wear is on the straps that go under the horse's belly and attach it—I think it could be easily repaired. The actual saddle is in great condition. Lovely leather decoration in a floral pattern. It is about 21.5 inches long, from the handle to the bottom of the stirrups. A wonderful saddle!

**Winning Bid:**

**$91.00**

**Ended:** 7/9/06
**History:** 11 bids
**Starting Bid:** $49.99
**Winner:** Lebanon, OR

**Viewed**
000241 X

# Mexican Saddle #100

## The Story

I am still in Hollywood finishing up the book—I even wrote the Hollywood bike story in Hollywood. Even stranger is the fact that we took a tour of Grauman's Chinese Theater this morning and the tour guide told us that Xavier Cugat had painted some of the artwork on the walls back in 1927. He also told us that not many people knew that this talented musician also painted.

I said, "How strange!" The first item in this book is a painting by Cugat and now I am writing the last story and his name is fresh in my mind. I feel like this book has come full circle and it is time to finish it. I always get a little sad when there are only a handful of stories left to write. I slow down a lot at the end because I want to keep writing and spending time reminiscing about my grandmother.

Back to business. This saddle was being sold (along with the Hollywood bike) as part of my house cleaning because it originally sat on a wooden horse that lived in my front entryway (or lobby, as my mom calls it). I bought this really neat piece of art at a charity sale in October of 2005 for $75.

I tried selling the horse and saddle together, but it never got any bids at auction and it had been parked in my eBay store for nine months—and also parked in my lobby. I hated to do it, but I finally decided to take the darling horse apart and sell the blanket and saddle separately to try and get some of my investment back.

Well, the saddle did sell for a nice amount—$91—which covered my $75 purchase price. I was then able to move the entire

heavy wooden horse out into the back yard as yard art. He is pretty cute!

Speaking of yard art, I am writing this sitting next to the pool at the Hotel Roosevelt. David Hockney painted the mural on the bottom of the pool where my kids are swimming and right above my head is the suite where Marilyn Monroe lived. Pretty neat. My mom just asked me if I think there are any famous people around us. "I'm sure that there are, but I don't have time to stare—I have a book to finish."

So my mom started chatting with Bruce, a member of the press who was at the hotel to cover the "On Hollywood" event. He asked what I do, and I said, "I am the Queen of Auctions." He said, "I have your DVD." I said, "No, you don't." And he said, "It's called 'Trash to Treasure' or something like that and I bought it from you at the LA Festival of Books."

Oh my gosh!—he really did have my DVD. My mom started cracking up, because while she was trying to find famous people, it turned out that she was sitting with someone slightly infamous in the eBay world—her own daughter. What I have learned is that everyone in Hollywood has a story, and this is mine.

# Afterword

It is hard to describe how I feel when I finish the last chapter of a book. There is still so much work to be done: finding the side photos, doing final read-throughs, making sure the stories fit on the page, and then waiting patiently for the books to come from the printer. After the writing is done, there is still another couple of months of work. So to say that I am happy or relieved when this part is done is not accurate.

I feel a sense of loss and I wonder if I have left anyone out. Should I have written about this friend instead of that friend? Should I have used this photo instead of that photo? Will anyone's feelings get hurt? Should I have told the story about my grandma and I on the Queen Mary? And so on. But most of all, I miss the chance to remember all the good times my grandmother and I had together. In fact, all the good times my friends and family and I have had.

And for the first time this year we are doing a galley proof. Not because we are smart, but because we had to. I set unrealistic expectations (like I always do) for how long it would take to finish this book. Why settle for what's here when I can shoot for the moon?

We debuted the book in New York at Book Expo America on June 1st, 2007. That meant that I needed to be done writing by April 15th, and instead I was in Nicaragua. But that is definitely a story for my next book. So to have copies available for autographing, we decided to print several hundred galleys.

Galley proofs are preliminary versions of a book. They are called that because in the days of hand-set type, the metal type would be set into a metal frame called a galley. Galleys are used today as advance reading copies for reviewers, magazines and libraries. They can also be used before a final press run to make sure you have no typos or other problems. So if you are lucky enough to have one of our advance reading copies, hang onto it—it may be worth money some day on eBay.

So whichever copy you have, thank you so much for reading my book. I really appreciate it! I really, really do! Now, do I sound a little like Sally Field?

I have started on my *4th 100 Best Things I've Sold on eBay*. At least the part where I gather data—just in case—I never know for sure what items will make the final cut. An author's work is never done!

I had this crazy idea to publish the 3rd book on 7-7-7, the 4th on 8-8-8 and so on until I finish the series on 12-12-12 with the *8th 100 Best Things I've Sold on eBay*. We will see.

I do appreciate all of you who write to us and send us your stories. We are still working on *The 100 Best Things You All Have Bought or Sold on eBay,* so if you have a story, please email it to Stories@TheQueenofAuctions.com.

God bless you and Godspeed.

Lyn

# Order now from The Queen of Auctions:

*The 100 Best Things I've Sold on eBay*—Paperback version—
The book that started the series—the original! ........... **$15.95 ea**

*More 100 Best Things I've Sold on eBay—Money Making Madness*
—Paperback. Lynn's Story continues. ......................... **$11.95 ea**

*i sell*—A 3-ring loose-leaf binder system for tracking your online
auction SALES  (200 pages w/tab dividers) ................. **$24.95 ea**

"Trash to Cash" Videos-Episodes 1 & 2 on one DVD—This
instructional video shows you how to do garage sales and sell on
eBay. Watch how $74 turns into $569 in cyberspace ....**$24.95 ea**

*How to Sell Antiques and Collectibles on eBay...and Make a Fortune!*
—This book teaches you the tricks and secrets you need to be
successful selling in this very lucrative category........... **$14.95 ea**

*The Unofficial Guide to Making Money on eBay*—Packed with tips
and insider information on every aspect of selling on eBay, this book
gives pros *and* amateurs an edge. ................................ **$18.95 ea**

Name_____

Address _____

City _____ State _____ Zip _____

Email _____ Telephone _____

$_____  Items
$_____  Shipping/Handling ($6.95 for 1st item and $2 each additional)
$_____  Sales Tax 7.75% CA Residents ONLY

**CHECKS** Payable to:
All Aboard Inc.
$_____  Total Enclosed
PO Box 14103
Palm Desert, CA  92255

To **CHARGE** your order, please fill in the information below:
_____ American Express _____ Discover _____ Visa _____ Master Card

Account No. _____ Expiration_____._____

Signature _____

**For more of Lynn's great teaching tools,** visit TheQueenOfAuctions.com
or order by **FAX** (760) 345-9441